The Visitation Quartet

Stephen Evans

For then my thoughts--from far where I abide--
Intend a zealous pilgrimage to thee.

> William Shakespeare

This is a work of fiction. The names, characters, places, and incidents are either the products of the author's imagination or are used fictitiously, and any resemblance to actual persons living or dead, business establishments, events, or locales is entirely coincidental.

For production permissions and rights, contact:
info@TimeBeingMedia.com

Copyright © 2024 by Stephen Evans. All rights reserved.

Book Layout ©2017 BookDesignTemplates.com

The Visitation Quartet Third Edition

ISBN: 978-1-953725-36-3

Contents

The Ghost Writer..3
Monuments 147
Tourists.. 265
Spooky Action at a Distance.................................. 399
About the Playwright 525
Books by Stephen Evans 527

Foreword

Leonardo DaVinci supposedly said *l'arte non è mai finita solo abbandonata*: Art is never finished, only abandoned. This volume is proof of that.

The Ghost Writer was started in the early 1980s and finished and first produced in the early 90s. Then it was rewritten and produced in 2013. Those versions were melded into the 2022 version.

Spooky Action at a Distance was begun the late 80s (the first three pages anyway). The first act was completed at The Greenbrier Hotel, a story told in another book. The second and third act came a few years later.

Monuments began its life in the summer of 2016, though I had had the idea in mind for years, ever since I read Robert D. Richardson's biography of Emerson. The extended version came in 2020, and achieved final (?0 form after reading *Solid Seasons* at the Thoreau Society Annual gathering in

Tourists found this form (I can't say was completed) in 2021.

So basically I've been writing this work for four decades. The plays have evolved over that time (this is the fourth edition), and I expect will continue to evolve as long as I do.

L'arte non è mai finita solo pubblicata.

STEPHEN EVANS

The Ghost Writer

A Play in Two Acts

STEPHEN EVANS

"Yet but three? Come one more."

William Shakespeare
A Midsummer Night's Dream

STEPHEN EVANS

For Will, Tom, Neil, and Fay – my Comedy Gurus.

Cast of Characters

KATE: A successful agent and attorney. She's fortyish, very bright, and passionate beneath hard-won knowledge.

MICHAEL: A gifted playwright who has never reached his artistic potential. 35 years old, he is Kate's current lover.

HARRY: A legendary New York producer struggling to regain his magic touch. Harry is a cross between Harold Hill and Harry Houdini. He is a survivor with a golden glint in his eye. At 60 years old, he is energetic, unprincipled, sexy, and Kate's ex.

WILL: The Ghost Writer.

Scene

A theater.

Time

The present.

STEPHEN EVANS

ACT I SCENE 1

Setting: A Broadway theater. Upstage center a door is built into the set.

At Rise: The set is decorated with decorated with banners, streamers, and balloons for an opening night party. But the stage is empty of people. Set pieces are scattered and overturned. Something bad has happened here.

Kate enters through the door, closing it tightly. She takes off her coat, revealing a glamorous evening gown. She throws her coat over an upside-down chair, then turns a table upright and sets out a bottle of champagne and three glasses. She pops open the champagne and pours all three.

Kate re-enters and begins, with obvious joy, to take down the decorations, stopping to pop a couple of balloons.

The door swings slowly open. She looks offstage.

KATE
Michael?

Hearing no answer, she goes to the door, looks out and sees no one. She closes it firmly, then returns to the decorations, popping the last balloon.

STEPHEN EVANS

The door slowly swings open again. More nervous, she goes to the door and looks out again.

KATE
Harry?

Again there's no answer. She again closes the door firmly, checks to make sure.

KATE
So may these outward shows be least themselves, the world is still deceived by ornaments.

Puzzled, and unable to understand why she has said these words, Kate leans with her back against the door. She hears turns her head to watch the knob on the door turn slowly, and the door inch open- creaking, naturally. She forces herself to look.

Michael's head appears in the doorway. They see each other and scream.)

KATE
Michael!

Michael looks around the set nervously.

MICHAEL
Is it safe?

KATE
It's 1:00 A.M. in New York City. You want safe, move to Connecticut.

Michael removes his coat, stands up an overturned coat rack, and hangs his coat up. He stares out into the audience.

MICHAEL
They'll hunt us down eventually.

KATE
Who?

MICHAEL
The audience.

KATE
There is that possibility. But you know what Harry says.
Imitating Harry's voice.
Never blame the audience, kid. All they do is sit there.

MICHAEL
That's true. That's all they did. Sit there. And sit there. And sit there. I think they may have stopped breathing. How much could you sit through?

KATE
About the first three hours.

MICHAEL
That was decent of you.

KATE
Well, I wanted to see how the first act ended.

MICHAEL
As I recall, in flames.

KATE
I would have stayed until the final curtain, but I forgot to pack a suitcase.

MICHAEL
Some agent. Opening night of my show and you won't even lie about how bad it is.

KATE
Can you call it an opening when it closes the same night?

MICHAEL
You're not helping.

She brings him a drink.

KATE
Anyway, I prefer the term personal representative. And be nice to me. I may have to support you.

MICHAEL
A few more of these and you'll definitely have to support me.

KATE
So. How do you feel?

MICHAEL
The same way I felt the last two times. Except I'm better at it with practice.

KATE
Makes sense.

MICHAEL
You know, at first, it was fine. People were enjoying themselves, smiling and laughing. I thought, this isn't so bad. And then it happened. Something that made my blood run cold.

KATE
What?

MICHAEL
The curtain went up.

KATE
Is there anything I can do?

MICHAEL
Could you shoot Harry?

KATE
I'm all out of silver bullets.

MICHAEL
Never mind.

KATE
Not listening, caught up in the idea
We could try a stake through his heart.

MICHAEL
Forget it.

KATE
But I doubt we could find it.

MICHAEL
I'm sorry I brought it up.

KATE
What?

MICHAEL
Just, thanks for listening.

KATE
That's what I'm here for.

MICHAEL
And thanks for not saying I told you so.

KATE
It never entered my mind.

She unveils a banner saying: I Told You So!

MICHAEL
Nice.

KATE
I saved it from the last time.

MICHAEL
I thought it looked familiar.

KATE
As far as I'm concerned, this is the best thing that could have happened, to both of us. You promised that if this show wasn't successful, you and I would go away together. Somewhere far away where you can get back to doing your kind of writing.

MICHAEL
Great. We're moving to Disneyland.

KATE
Almost. I was thinking maybe L.A. You could try screenwriting.

MICHAEL
Hollywood. What a concept! There would be no limit to the amount of money I could squander.

KATE
I'm serious. You should think about it. Actually, I've been thinking about it for a while now. I've been offered an executive position with a studio—top budgets, choice of projects, everything I could want. And they said I could bring you in with me.

MICHAEL
I see.

KATE
So, what do you think?

MICHAEL
Are you going?

KATE
I asked what you think?

MICHAEL
I think you should go.

KATE
I see. What about you?

MICHAEL
I'm a playwright.

KATE
Look, I know lately things haven't been right between us.

MICHAEL
That has nothing to do with it.

KATE
Maybe, with a fresh start somewhere...

MICHAEL
Kate, I wish I could tell you what you want to hear. You deserve it. But I can't.

KATE
Okay, maybe you could teach, I don't know. The important thing is that we'll be there, and Harry won't.

MICHAEL
You can't blame this all on Harry.

KATE
Why not? Everyone else does. Admit it: If it wasn't for Harry, you never would have touched the kind of material I saw tonight. I don't understand how he talks people into these things. Not just you- everybody, including me. I've been with him since I got out of law school, and I can't tell you why I put up with it.

MICHAEL
I can. There are two reasons.

KATE
Enlighten me.

MICHAEL
First, he used to be one of the most successful producers on Broadway.

KATE
Ancient history. What's the second reason?

MICHAEL
The second reason you know as well as I do. He can make anything sound reasonable. He could sell weight loss centers in Third World countries. In fact, I think he tried it.

KATE
That is exactly why you have to get away from him. He is manipulative, insensitive, and totally without any sense of decency.

MICHAEL
I like him too.

KATE
Michael, I know he's your oldest friend. He's mine, too. But you've outgrown him. It's time to move on.

MICHAEL
I know. I know.
    She looks at him skeptically.
I know!

KATE
Promise me you'll tell him tonight?

MICHAEL
I promise.

KATE
Then let's break out the champagne. We have something to celebrate after all.

At this point, Harry bursts in. He too is in formal attire, though his is rumpled.

HARRY
Break out the champagne! We have something to celebrate after all.

MICHAEL
What are you talking about?

HARRY
The show, of course. A triumph of the first magnitude.
They stare at him.

HARRY
Okay, maybe not the first magnitude. But a triumph, nonetheless.

MICHAEL
You really have lost it this time, Harry. The show was a disaster. It sank with all hands. There were no survivors.

HARRY
You're over-reacting.

MICHAEL
Were you at the same opening night I was?

KATE
Can you call it an opening when it closes the same night?

MICHAEL
You're not helping!

KATE
Sorry.
> *Bringing them each a glass of champagne*

KATE
Here. This is the extent of my commiseration for tonight.

KATE
> *To Harry*

If you need me, I'll be in the office working on your bankruptcy. Take your time. By the way, watch out for that curtain.

> *She exits.*

MICHAEL
Now you tell me.

HARRY
I still don't think it was that bad. During the first act, people were smiling and laughing.

MICHAEL
They were throwing paper airplanes at the actors.

HARRY
Then at intermission, half the audience left.

MICHAEL
The lucky half.

HARRY
Maybe their babysitters had to be home early.

MICHAEL
I've heard babysitters have a very strong union.

HARRY
I'm just trying to cheer you up.

He makes another drink, very strong, and gives it to Michael

HARRY
Actually, Mike, I wasn't going to tell you this until tomorrow. But, in my professional judgment based on my 33 years on Broadway...

MICHAEL
Yes?

HARRY
The show was a disaster. It sank with all hands. There were no survivors.

MICHAEL
An eloquent eulogy to an excruciating evening.

HARRY
Now we can't take this too hard.

MICHAEL
You know, that's true. No matter how hard we take this, it's not too hard.

HARRY
That's not what I mean. Theater is a risky business.

MICHAEL
What business? All we do is lose money. It's more like a charity program for lawyers.

HARRY
With a lawyer like Kate, is that so bad?
Puzzled
She seems to be taking this rather well.

MICHAEL
She's imagining how many people are going to sue us in the morning. And she's also thinking that I'll be able to stay home now and clean the apartment. This is the most depressing night of my life since our last opening night. I hate feeling like this. Why do we do it, anyway? Why do we put ourselves through this?

HARRY
Maybe we could write a book about it.

MICHAEL
There's something very wrong with the whole process.

HARRY
We could write a book about the whole process.

MICHAEL
Maybe we're fooling ourselves.

HARRY
We could write a book about fools.

MICHAEL
Maybe the magic is gone.

HARRY
We could call it Magic Fools.

MICHAEL
All the pain and the suffering and the lost time. That's the worst. The time.

HARRY
Harry looks at Michael's watch
2:15. Or maybe we could open a clinic for failures.

MICHAEL
Time and failure.

HARRY
Our motto could be: Nobody knows failure like we do.

MICHAEL
Nobody knows the trouble I've seen. Nothing ever seems to work out right anymore. We should have known. We did know. But still we wasted all that money, all that- time.

HARRY
Again Harry looks at Michael's watch
2:16. We could have counseling centers across the country. Failures Anonymous. Or, Failure Associates. How do you do, I'm Harry Skidmore, senior failure consultant.

MICHAEL
The question is: Why?

HARRY
What?

MICHAEL
What?

HARRY
What did you say?

MICHAEL
I said why?

HARRY
Oh.
Pause
Why what?

MICHAEL
Let's work backwards on this one. You said why what to my what asking what you said which means that you said why what to my original why meaning that you want to know why I said why?

Pause

HARRY
What?

MICHAEL
I thought it was perfectly clear.

Pause

HARRY
What?

MICHAEL
What I said.

HARRY
Which what?

MICHAEL
No, we're entering a whole new dimension here. We'd better quit while we're ahead.

Pause

HARRY
Ahead of what?

MICHAEL
Let me put it this way: Why do...we do...what we do? I sound like Frank Sinatra.

HARRY
We do it because we have to.

MICHAEL
Why?

HARRY
Why what?

MICHAEL
Don't start that again. Why do we have to do it?

HARRY
We need to.

MICHAEL
But why?

HARRY
Slightly annoyed by the obviousness of it all
To live out the fullest expression of our lives, making each act a tiny catalyst in the combustion of infinite beauty.

MICHAEL
Oh. Did you make that up?

HARRY
I think it was in a Lite Beer commercial.

MICHAEL
Why did I ask?

HARRY
Ask what? Just kidding! Anyway it's a stupid question. There is no "why". We do it because it's what we do. I am a producer. You are a writer. So, we produce and write.

MICHAEL
How simple life is for the tautologically challenged. In that case, I have another question: what do we do now?

HARRY
We move on.

MICHAEL
No.

HARRY
Continue.

MICHAEL
Sorry.

HARRY
Try, try again?

MICHAEL
Wrong. Harry, sit down.

HARRY
He is sitting
Okay.

MICHAEL
I've been meaning to talk to you about this for a long time, but I could never figure out how to say it.

HARRY
You can say anything to me.

MICHAEL
Okay. Harry, this is the third time in a row that we have failed to keep a show open past opening night. I think that's a clue. Someone is telling us to stop.

HARRY
Yeah, the New York Times.

Michael reacts.

HARRY
Sorry. So we've hit a few rough spots. It happens to everyone. You can't forget everything we've been through just because we're having an off period.

MICHAEL
We're not having an off period. We're off. Period. And I haven't forgotten what you and I been through together. It was a miracle. But one miracle is all you get in life, Harry.

We've had ours. We shouldn't be greedy. I mean it's not like we need the money anymore.

HARRY
Bite your tongue.

MICHAEL
But we have to face the fact that we can't produce anything decent. We never were artistic, but at least we were clever. Now we're—what did they say—obvious. Mindless. Trite. Garbage. Tell me when to stop. Let's face it! You and I are through. I can't write what you want anymore. I'm empty. Drained. It's time to pack up, go home, teach freshman English at some small Midwestern college that does "Our Town" every spring. Don't you see?

The weight of this sad time we must obey,
speak what we feel, not what we ought to say.

HARRY
There's no need to get literary. I feel bad enough as it is.

MICHAEL
I don't know why I said that.

HARRY
You need sleep.

MICHAEL
I need time. To myself.

HARRY
We'll talk about it tomorrow. I'll fix you my special tonic, and then you'll sleep the sleep of the damned.

MICHAEL
It wouldn't surprise me.

HARRY
What time did I say it was?

MICHAEL
Thou art so fat-witted with drinking of old sack, and unbuttoning thee after supper, and sleeping upon benches after noon, that thou hast forgotten that which thou wouldst truly know. What a devil hast thou to do with the time of day? Unless hours were cups of sack and minutes capons, and clocks the tongues of bawds, and dials the signs of sleeping houses, and the blessed sun himself a fair hot wench in flame coloured taffeta, I see no reason why thou shouldst be so superfluous as to demand the time of day.

HARRY
If you don't want to tell me, just say so.

MICHAEL
Henry IV, Part 1.

HARRY
What?

MICHAEL
That was Hal's speech to Falstaff in Act 1, scene 2 of Henry IV, Part 1. Or was it Act 1, scene 1 of Henry the IV, Part 2?

HARRY
It could be Rocky 5 for all I know.

MICHAEL
I love that speech. That's one of my favorite speeches.

HARRY
Shakespeare. Now there was a great operator.

MICHAEL
But it's not what I was going to say.

HARRY
He knew just what his audiences wanted.

MICHAEL
I once thought I was going to be the next Shakespeare.

HARRY
A little blood, a little sex, a little more blood, and he had a hit. Today he'd be the president of a network.

MICHAEL
The next Shakespeare. What a laugh.

HARRY
Too bad Old Will isn't here now. We could use a little influence. Influence...

Harry gets THE IDEA, and begins working it out, following Michael around the room as if measuring him.

MICHAEL
Lately, when I'm working, I feel like Dr. Frankenstein. Whatever I write comes sneaking up behind me with murder in its eyes.

Michael looks behind himself, sees Harry, and starts.

It isn't worth it anymore, Harry. I'm going home.

HARRY
I know.

MICHAEL
I mean it. I'm heading west into the sunset.

HARRY
I think that's best. You've been through enough. Seeing your work torn apart by unfeeling audiences, insensitive critics, and, I admit it, greedy producers.

MICHAEL
You're obviously plotting something, and I don't want to know what it is. What is it?

HARRY
I'm just agreeing with you. It's time to go home.

MICHAEL
It is?

HARRY
It is. It's time to return to the source.

MICHAEL
The source?

HARRY
Yes, the source. As in:
> *Harry makes a big gesture*

The SOURCE. We need a return to that which made the theater great in days of yore.

MICHAEL
You mean tap-dancing?

HARRY
No. Farther yore than that.

MICHAEL
I know this is a mistake, but—what are you talking about?

HARRY
Releasing his excitement

Mike, in a little while, people are going to be throwing money at us. We'll have to hire people to count the people counting it.

MICHAEL
Harry, calm down.

HARRY
Our next show will be the show of the century!

MICHAEL
Harry, there isn't going to be a next show. After tonight's show, they won't even let us drive down Broadway. Besides, why would anyone want to see a new show from us?

HARRY
Because we're not going to write it.

MICHAEL
That's a good start. Who is?

HARRY
William Shakespeare.

MICHAEL
Harry, William Shakespeare is dead.

HARRY
That's what makes it so spectacular.

MICHAEL
I can't argue with that. Well, if it's okay with him, it's okay with me. Just remember that I'm leaving.

HARRY
You can't leave.

MICHAEL
Why not?

HARRY
He only talks to you.

MICHAEL
Death is no excuse for being anti-social.

HARRY
Can you roll your eyes?

MICHAEL
No, but I can roll my 'R's.

HARRY
Work on it. Can you moan?

MICHAEL
This is getting personal.

HARRY
Never mind, we'll get a sound man.

MICHAEL
Neither of us will qualify.

HARRY
Now, when the reporters come–

MICHAEL
Reporters?

HARRY
The public has a right to know about something as momentous as this. When the reporters come, you may have to moan and roll yours eyes at the same time. So start practicing.
  Michael moans and rolls his eyes in disbelief

HARRY
That was good. Keep practicing.

MICHAEL
Stop. Don't say any more. I want to go back to the beginning so that I can prepare my insanity defense.

HARRY
Fair enough.

MICHAEL
Okay. Now. You and I are going to do a play, a play written by William Shakespeare.

                    HARRY
Not just a play. A <u>new</u> play.

                    MICHAEL
A new play, that no one has ever seen before, written by Shakespeare.

                    HARRY
Right.

                    MICHAEL
Only, now this is just a guess on my part, Shakespeare isn't really going to write this play.

                    HARRY
Right.

                    MICHAEL
And if Shakespeare isn't going to write this play written by Shakespeare, who is?

                    BOTH
You are.

                    MICHAEL
Right.

                    HARRY
I'll make it simple.

                    MICHAEL
I can't wait to hear this.

                    HARRY
You are going to write a play. A very, very good play. The best play that anyone has written for years and years. Real Art stuff. We are going to tell the world that Shakespeare is writing this play through you. A spiritual connection. A voice from the other world. It happens all the time. There's a woman in England who writes music by Mozart and

Beethoven. Only she can't read a note. She just hears it in her head.

MICHAEL
You should call her. We could do a musical.

HARRY
You know... no, next time maybe. Anyway, this is big time stuff now. What's it called? Tunneling.

MICHAEL
I think that's Channeling.

HARRY
Whatever. Besides, Shakespeare was always writing about ghosts.

MICHAEL
How would you know?

HARRY
I am not totally alliterative. I'm telling you this is genius. This may be the greatest idea I have ever had.

MICHAEL
Now there's an intense competition. Harry, even you can't be serious about this.

HARRY
I know we can pull it off. You said yourself that no one would touch one of our shows. But how can they turn down Shakespeare?

MICHAEL
How are you going to get the money? Who in his or her right mind would even listen to you long enough to let you explain it?

HARRY
You.

MICHAEL
Harry, be sensible. Suppose I could write something good enough to have been written by Shakespeare. Who would believe it was his and not mine?

HARRY
Look at it this way. If you did write something that good, who would believe it was yours and not his?

MICHAEL
You've never stooped to telling the truth before.

HARRY
I lost my head. Look at it another way. Suppose what you write isn't so terrific. He's been dead 500 years; he's bound to be a little rusty.
Serious
I know we haven't done too well together recently...

MICHAEL
Shall I count the slashes on my wrist?

HARRY
And I know it's my fault. My style just doesn't work anymore. The audiences are different now. They don't want what I have to give. They see it on TV, in reruns, and they fall all over it. But put it on Broadway... I don't know. But I'm thinking, maybe they'll want you, if I let you do what you do best. You deserve that opportunity. And I need to be the one to give it to you. Does that make sense?

MICHAEL
Yeah. I think so.

HARRY
You know, tonight I was sitting in the house watching the show. But I couldn't keep my mind on it.

MICHAEL
You and the first thirty rows.

HARRY
Something happened, something very small, and now nothing's the same for me.

MICHAEL
What?

HARRY
It's silly. But I keep thinking about it. It was during the show. I saw you.

MICHAEL
That must have been a shock.

HARRY
Demonstrating
And you took your program and folded it down the center.

MICHAEL
Paper airplanes, I told you.

HARRY
And then you very carefully, very neatly, tore it in half. And I knew it was the end.

MICHAEL
Harry?

HARRY
And I won't fight it, if you'll do one thing for me—let me give you this last show. Let me give you this chance. Look, we don't have to be out of here until tomorrow. What better place to write about Shakespeare than in a theater? Just try. One night.

MICHAEL
Harry?

HARRY
I'll make a deal with you. One night, and if you don't think it will work. Then I'll go. I'll... retire. You'll be free. Don't decide now. Just think about it. Okay?

MICHAEL
I'll think about it.

HARRY
Thanks. Well. I guess I better go.

MICHAEL
Meaningfully
Where will you go?

HARRY
Misunderstanding
To the library. It's time that Shakespeare and I met quill to quill.

He leaves

MICHAEL
**This thought is as a death which cannot choose
But weep to have that which it fears to lose.**
I think I'm having a midsummer day's nightmare.

Kate enters.

KATE
He's gone?

MICHAEL
Yes.

KATE
Was he angry?

MICHAEL
No, I wouldn't say he was angry.

KATE
Did you break it to him gently?

MICHAEL
Gently. Yeah. I'd say gently.

KATE
I'm glad you were gentle. How gentle were you?

MICHAEL
Gentle. Very gentle. Extremely gentle. So gentle that he may not even realize that I told him.

KATE
You didn't tell him.

MICHAEL
I tried. I just couldn't. You know, it took him all of three minutes to recover. He's already working on our next play. I tried to tell him. He wouldn't listen. Oh, the good part is that I'm not writing it.

KATE
Who is?

MICHAEL
Let's just say he's bringing in a ghost writer.

KATE
A ghost writer? For whom?

MICHAEL
A ghost. Harry's got this idea that I am going to collaborate with the spirit of William Shakespeare.

KATE
Michael, do you ever just stop and think?

MICHAEL
I don't think so.

KATE
I don't mean think, I mean... just let your mind go blank.

MICHAEL
Oh. Frequently.

KATE
Somebody once told me that, when you let your mind go blank, the first thing you think about is the thing you want most. After you let your mind drift, what's your first thought?

MICHAEL
You.

KATE
That's a good answer. Now tell the truth.

MICHAEL
Well, if you're going to be picky... food.

KATE
Why food?

MICHAEL
My mind only goes blank when I'm hungry.

KATE
You're always hungry.

MICHAEL
My mind goes blank a lot.

KATE
Try to be serious.

MICHAEL
I'm trying.

KATE
You certainly are. Don't you ever think about what's important to you?

MICHAEL
I did when I was young.

KATE
You're still young.

MICHAEL
I didn't say it was a long time ago.

KATE
Fine. So tell me what's important to you.
A long pause
Did you think about food again?

MICHAEL
Not until you brought it up.

KATE
I'm sorry. Don't think about food.

MICHAEL
You can't not think about something unless you think about not thinking about it. So if I don't think about it I'm thinking about it.

KATE
Okay, go ahead and think about it.

MICHAEL
Thanks, I'm not hungry.

KATE
You're being purposely evasive.

MICHAEL
I just can't talk about these things with you.

KATE
I see. Can you tell me why?

MICHAEL
It's like the candles on your birthday cake. You blow them out and make a wish. But if you tell anyone, it won't come true.

KATE
That's not it. I know why you won't talk to me. I know why Harry can talk you into anything. You can afford to fail by other people's standards. But you're afraid to let anyone judge you by your own. Do you know why I got into this business? Because my talent is seeing talent, and finding a way to make it grow. You have as much talent as anyone I've ever worked with, and it's all going to waste. Whose fault is that?

MICHAEL
Not yours.

KATE
Damn right it's not mine. So why is it that I can't help but blame myself? I should have kept things strictly business. Then I was just losing money.

MICHAEL
You're just soft-hearted, that's all.

KATE
About you, maybe. About nothing else in this world.

MICHAEL
How about Harry?

KATE
I said this world, not the underworld.

MICHAEL
I wish you could explain to me why you feel the way you do about him. Nobody can get to you like he can.

KATE
You do all right.

MICHAEL
No. I make you angry. Harry makes you desperate. Why?

KATE
What has he told you?

MICHAEL
Not much. He told me that one night at a party you both got drunk and you ended up sleeping together, and that you've never been the same since.

KATE
It's not true.

MICHAEL
What's not true? That you slept together or that it was only one night? It's obvious you've never been the same.

KATE
Stop it.

MICHAEL
Why? Feeling desperate?

KATE
If I am, it's for you.

MICHAEL
Tell me what he meant to you.

KATE
I can't.

MICHAEL
Well. I guess that makes us even. Harry will be back here any minute now. I don't think he realized that there are very few libraries open at two o'clock in the morning. So, what should I tell him? Or is there something you'd like to tell him?
Pause
He says if I do this, he'll leave.

KATE
Maybe, in some way I don't understand, I'm holding you back as much as he is.

MICHAEL
No. You don't know...

KATE
Just do me a favor. Don't follow him all your life. You want to know who the real ghost writer around here is? It's the one who died the day you met him.

MICHAEL
Kate, I...

There's a noise offstage, someone tripping over something.

KATE
Go to your room.

MICHAEL
Yes, Mother.

KATE
I'll handle this. I just want a little privacy.

MICHAEL
A la Groucho
Why didn't you say so?

Kate glares

MICHAEL
I'm going, I'm going.

KATE
Good idea.

He leaves. Harry enters

KATE
How was the library?

HARRY
Closed.

KATE
They don't keep the same hours as adult bookstores.

HARRY
Did Mike tell you why I went to the library?

KATE
He did.

HARRY
What did you do with the body?

KATE
The same thing I'm going to do with yours. Harry—

HARRY
I know what you're going to say. You're going to say I'm a rotten devious scheming meddler who doesn't deserve to be associated with a real talent like Mike.

KATE
Right.

HARRY
And then you're going to say that I'm ruining his career, like I almost ruined yours.

KATE
Exactly.

HARRY
I didn't mean to.

KATE
What am I going to do with you? You're like the Pied Piper, Harry. These kids come to you, fresh and eager and naive like I was, and they follow you until they drown. I was lucky. I learned to swim. But he won't. He'll drown unless you help.

HARRY
Did I ever tell you how we met?

KATE
I know how we met. I was there.

HARRY
How Mike and I met.

KATE
You must have. There is very little that goes on in your brain that doesn't eventually come out of your mouth—

HARRY
He was still in college–

KATE
At least twice.

HARRY
It was right after you left me.

KATE
Which time?

HARRY
The last, I think.

KATE
That was my best.

HARRY
There was a professor who was a friend of mine.

KATE
Past tense I note.

HARRY
Every year he'd drag me down to this little hole in the wall theater across from the campus to see his latest prodigy. I don't know why I went, except you never know, right?

KATE
Right. You never know when you're going to find a coed who'd just love to meet a Broadway producer.

HARRY
Well, that too. It was an evening of one act plays. I fell asleep mid-way through act one. All of them. And then these words started drifting in and out of my dream.

He pulls a crumpled piece of paper out of his wallet.

HARRY
It's a little hard to read now. Where are my glasses?
He puts them on.
He said, this guy in the play said:
Reading a little but knowing a lot.
We were never happy together. Not once. At least, she was never happy with me. But I always thought that we were really happy being unhappy together. I mean, we were probably going to be unhappy anyway. So why not be unhappy with someone you love? That's what love is all about-sharing your unhappiness together.

KATE
That sounds like us.

HARRY
That's what I thought.

Pause

HARRY
Anyway, I thought, how does this kid who's never been anywhere know how I feel this exact moment? I had to meet the playwright. Anyway, what I'm really trying to say is, it's all your fault.

KATE
My fault?

HARRY
Yes. If you hadn't left me, I wouldn't have been feeling that way and I wouldn't have asked to meet him.

KATE
I see.

HARRY
I wonder what would have happened to him. You know? If I had shown up one week earlier or one week later...

KATE
We'll never know.

HARRY
I guess. I need your help, Kate. I want your help.

KATE
Is that all you want?

HARRY
It's against the rules to know what you want until it's too late to get it.

KATE
Break the rules. You're good at it.

HARRY
I used to think so. Kate, I'm trying to learn to be one of the good guys. I don't know if I can. I'm not sure why I want to. But I need help.

He takes her hand

HARRY
I need to make it up to him. I need to make it up to me. And to you.

KATE
Calling
Michael!

He enters.

MICHAEL
No sign of a struggle.

KATE
Do you know you talk in your sleep? You do. You talk a lot. But I can never understand the words. And I wonder. I wonder if you're writing in your sleep the words you should be writing when you're awake. I know it sounds ridiculous. But you know what's even more ridiculous? I sit there listening, sometimes all night, with a pencil and a notebook, trying to catch the words. I never can. But I try. Because I think someday I'm going to understand those words. I'm going to write them down. And when I do I'm going to wake you up and show them to you, and you're going to see what you can really do. I'd give everything for that.

MICHAEL
I don't understand...

                    KATE
You're doing the play.

                    MICHAEL
What? But you said...

                    KATE
I know what I said, but I've thought it over and I think you should do one more. Only this time you are going to write the right words, your words.

   She turns to Harry.

                    KATE
From now on, I'm going to see that no one, not Harry, not me, not the Ghost of Shakespeare himself, comes between you and your work.

   She turns back to Michael

                    KATE
I'm going to live, eat, sleep, breathe, laugh, cry, and everything else I can think of with you, until you are through with this play, and anything else that holds you to the life you're living now.

   She turns back to Harry

                    KATE
Okay, this is the way it's going to be...

   She moves away to talk to Harry. Michael looks at her

                    MICHAEL
**Perhaps he loves you now,
and now no soil or cautel doth besmirch
the virtue of his will; but you must fear,
his greatness weighed, his will is not his own,
for he himself is subject to his birth.**

                    KATE
Did you say something?

                   MICHAEL
It's a mystery to me.

   Blackout

Stephen Evans

Act I Scene 2

Setting: The Theater

Time: A few hours later.

At Rise: Michael is seated down stage right, laptop perched on something it shouldn't be, a printer not far away.

Michael leans back in his chair, and shoots wads of paper at a hoop above a shredder. Each time he makes one we hear the shredder grinding away. He makes one, two, then misses. He gets up, retrieves it again, shoots again, and misses again. He picks up the can, sits down on the floor, and begins to cover himself with the paper.

Harry enters, carrying a large trash can.

HARRY
I met a man from the Sanitation department downstairs. If I empty this one more time, I have to join the Union.

MICHAEL
Better trash in the can than on the stage. Think of it as a humanitarian service. You're saving the world from this.

He uncrumples a page and reads

MICHAEL
Yesterdays, yesterdays, yesterdays
Flee in frantic folly from fickle fears

to the last earful of contorted rhyme.

> HARRY

Just think: a tree died for that.

> MICHAEL

I'm getting threatening phone calls from Smokey the Bear.

> HARRY

By the way, I found some books for you. Consider it research.
> *Taking the paper*

What does this mean?

> MICHAEL

I have to write it. Do I have to know what it means?

> HARRY

I was just wondering. I think writing is interesting.

> MICHAEL

So do I. I wish I knew how it was done. I'm not a writer, I'm a lumberjack.

> HARRY

It's a little early for your 3 AM depression.

> MICHAEL

Can't I go home?

> HARRY

This is a theater. You are home. Besides, what could possibly be more inspiring?

> MICHAEL

A bed.

> HARRY

There's one in the dressing room backstage. You can sleep for an hour.

MICHAEL
Really?

HARRY
After you finish the first act.

MICHAEL
You're one of the good guys, Harry.

HARRY
That's what I keep telling everyone. You know I don't like to waste time, kid. Can you at least tell me the story?

MICHAEL
It's an old English legend, the story of the Unicorn.

HARRY
Unicorn?

MICHAEL
So the story is, a young boy in the forest thinks he sees a unicorn.

HARRY
Isn't that an animal?

MICHAEL
The kid tells his parents, who punish him for lying.

HARRY
Does it have to be an animal show?

MICHAEL
But the kid cries and cries that he's telling the truth.

HARRY
I hate animal shows.

MICHAEL
So, to calm him down, his parents go to see. At first, they can't see anything.

HARRY
You always have to watch where you're walking backstage.

MICHAEL
But the kid believes so strongly that soon the parents begin to see as well.

HARRY
Besides.

MICHAEL
And when all three of them believe, the unicorn is born into the world. Great story, huh?

HARRY
Unicorns are expensive.

MICHAEL
Harry, the unicorn is a mythical beast.

HARRY
Great, it'll be twice as expensive. Think of something else.

MICHAEL
There is nothing else. This is it. I'm desperate. In all of this paper, there is not one line that is worthy of comparison to Shakespeare. Not one. I think we're wasting our time.

HARRY
The problem is that you are trying to write like Shakespeare, and you can't. Shakespeare never wrote "Shakespeare", he wrote plays. Plays about people. You remember people.

MICHAEL
Vaguely. I'm a playwright remember. We're not allowed out in public.

HARRY
Don't worry so much.

MICHAEL
Every time I listen to you, I end up losing something. What am I going to lose this time?

HARRY
I don't know. What've you got left? Stop worrying! Just do it. You been on my back for ten years to let you write something artistic. So now's the time.

MICHAEL
It's not that easy.

HARRY
You know why it's not easy? Because it's impossible. You're sitting here thinking "Wow, I've got to come with some real art." Can't be done. You think Shakespeare did that? No way. First, he comes up with a story. Maybe he makes it up, maybe he steals it. Usually, he steals it, but from somebody dead, so he's got no problems. Then, he finds some people. He puts the people into the story. If it's a sad story, he finds sad people. If it's a funny story, he finds funny people. Then, he makes sure someone falls in love, and somebody dies, usually from falling in love. He throws in a witch, or maybe a fairy, then at the end he chops off someone's head. Bingo- he's got a hit. The whole process takes maybe a week. You think he labored over every line? No way. The man had deadlines.

MICHAEL
So what are you saying?

HARRY
What am I saying? I'm saying stop trying to please some dead guy. Just please yourself. I know you. I've been beating these artistic notions out of you for a long time now. As soon as I leave the room they come back, that's time-tested. Trust me. You already know what you want to be when you grow up. So be it.

MICHAEL
Okay. You know you should have been a preacher.

HARRY
I think I am. You should have been a writer.

MICHAEL
I think I am. I must have forgotten.

HARRY
So write. Stop wasting my time with questions.

Kate enters with bags of Chinese food.

KATE
Hi. What's going on?

MICHAEL
Sermon number 37.

KATE
I'm sorry I missed it. What was it about?

MICHAEL
Amnesia.

KATE
What?

HARRY
Loss. Of memory.

MICHAEL
Was that it?

HARRY
I forget.

KATE
Why don't you forget about that for a while and help me with the food.

MICHAEL

With pleasure.

Kate and Michael exit. Harry walks over to the desk, picks up a copy of King Lear, and begins to read.

                    HARRY
This is the excellent foppery of the world, that,
          He stops reading.
when we are sick in fortune,- often the surfeit of our own behavior- we make guilty of our disasters the sun, the moon, and the stars; as if we were villains by necessity, fools by heavenly compulsion, knaves, thieves and treachers by spherical predominance, drunkards, liars, and adulterers by an enforced obedience of planetary influence; and all that we are evil in, by a divine thrusting on.

Boy, he really hits you over the head with it, doesn't he?
          He looks offstage
Need any help? I didn't think so. That's okay. I'm not hurt.

I'm starting to care about things. That's not normal.

But don't give it a second thought. Don't let the fact that I'm depressed and all alone influence you. I don't even want you back.

   Kate enters.

                    KATE
I'm back.

                    HARRY
What?

                    KATE
I'm back. I went out. And now I'm back.

                    HARRY
Oh.

   He laughs.

KATE
What's so funny?

HARRY
Wishful thinking. There's a little of that in the best of us.

KATE
You are made of nothing else.

HARRY
**True, I talk of dreams,
which are the children of an idle brain,
begot of nothing but vain fantasy;
which is as thin of substance as the air.**

KATE
We've all got Shakespeare on the brain lately.

HARRY
I must be memorizing this stuff self-consciously as I read.

KATE
Harry, are you all right? You seem almost...human.

HARRY
It's the aging process, I guess. I feel like a fine wine in a leaky barrel.

KATE
She sits
Well, don't drip on me, please.

HARRY
There is one consolation that comes with age. You learn to see through your own illusions.

KATE
And stop trying to play on my sympathy. It's all played out.

HARRY

Wouldn't put it past me. But I know better. You need him. He needs you. And neither one of you has much use for me.

He sits next to her.

KATE

Wrong again, as usual. I need someone. He needs something. And we both happen to be standing in for the other. The past is repeating itself. It's like watching home movies, all blurry and too fast and too familiar.

HARRY

What's wrong?

KATE

I can't tell you.

HARRY

You can tell me anything. You know I never listen.

KATE

Well, in that case. When Michael and I are alone together, he looks at me as if I'm a ghost. You know, something from his past that didn't know when to leave. I want to do what's best for him. But I'm afraid that once I do, he'll be gone.

HARRY

I think we've found something in common.

KATE

It must be the end of the world.

HARRY

It's possible. Kate?

KATE

Don't say my name.

HARRY
Why not?

KATE
Because I really want someone to hold me now and I couldn't stand it if it was you.

There is a pause, in which they both stay still. Slowly, almost unconsciously, she leans her head on his shoulder. There is another pause.

KATE
I hate myself for this.

HARRY
Hate me instead. You have more practice at it.

KATE
That's the truth.

Michael enters. They don't notice. He stands and listens, smiling

KATE
Harry, is he going to leave us?

HARRY
Everyone leaves everyone eventually.

KATE
Do they?

HARRY
I hope not.

KATE
You know, when you're feeling old like this, it makes me feel young. I'm beginning to remember things myself.

HARRY
What kind of things?

KATE
Childish things.

HARRY
Those are good things to remember. I remember the first time I saw you. I remember the first time I kissed you. I remember the first time we-

KATE
Stop remembering!

HARRY
Sorry.

KATE
I suppose I should go back out and help with the food.

Michael exits.

HARRY
I suppose you should.

A pause. No one moves.

KATE
Have I left yet?

HARRY
Afraid not.

KATE
I didn't think so. Start remembering again. What happened to us?

HARRY
We loved not wisely but too well.

KATE
That tells me a lot.

HARRY
Actually, you never really loved me. You were just infatuated with my glamour, wealth, and good looks.

KATE
That's true.

HARRY
It is?

KATE
I don't know. It sounds familiar.

HARRY
The sad thing is you never did love me.

KATE
I never cried over any man but you.

HARRY
That's a healthy definition of love.

KATE
How would you know? No, it wasn't that I didn't love you. But even love wasn't worth getting walked over every day. I deserved better.

HARRY
I know.

KATE
I hate that. You always stop fighting just when I get mad enough to tell the truth.

HARRY
I always did have great timing, down to the last exquisite slam of the taxi door. Though as I recall, it was your hand on the door handle.

KATE
Survival seemed important.

HARRY
At my age, I knew better.

KATE
At your age, it was less likely.

HARRY
You're all heart.

KATE
I was once.

HARRY
You still are.

KATE
I still am.

She laughs a little.

HARRY
What?

KATE
Shaking her head.
I'd better help with the food.
Pause. This time he slides unconsciously toward Kate, and they kiss.
Have I left yet?

HARRY
No question about it. We both have. Left our senses.

Getting up, breaking the mood.
How did you do today?

    KATE

Harry, I...

    HARRY

From now on, you and I have one rule. We don't hurt him.

    KATE

Really?

    HARRY

We're talking survival now too.

    KATE

The question is whose? Damn it, I've worked hard for this crisis. I'm entitled to it. I just prefer to panic in private. I mean, look at me. I have a great career, plenty of money, even love, of a sort. Everything I'm supposed to want. So why do I always feel so disappointed? You want to hear paranoia? I just know that, on my deathbed, just before I go, I'll finally discover my reason for living. I don't think I'd mind living my life in ignorance if I thought I could die in ignorance too. But I just know that when I'm on my last legs, some joker is going to come whisper the secret of the ages in my ear. And at that moment, when it's too late, I'll know my life is a waste. That scares me more than death. But I don't know what to do about it. I'm no saint. I'm not going to spend my life in Calcutta. I think people who do are wonderful, but that's not me. And I'm no great artist. Day after day, I work with people whose talent is unimaginable to me. As human beings, you wouldn't want to meet them on the subway, but as artists, they have this gift from the universe that makes their life clear, to me at least, if not to them. But I can't run off to Tahiti to paint. I have trouble with crayons. So, what's left?

> HARRY
> Here's a radical thought. How about a home and a family?

> KATE
> Maybe that's it. Maybe it's that simple.

> HARRY
> From what I hear, it's not so simple.

> KATE
> You know what I mean. But I ask myself: is that what they're going to whisper to me at the end of my life? You are alive so that your children may have life. Where is the meaning in that? Where is the sense? Where is anything but the mindless repetition of a biological imperative?

> HARRY
> Personally, I think there's a lot to be said for mindless repetition.

> KATE
> And biological imperatives, I know. But is that why we're alive?

> HARRY
> Why does everyone think there has to be a why?

> KATE
> We need them.

> HARRY
> Then make up your own.

> KATE
> That's something you would say. I don't mind playing the game, I just want someone to show me the rules.

> HARRY
> Don't look at me.

KATE
I can't help it. I never could. But what if. What if we're finally ready to show each other?

HARRY
You'd be wasting your time with me. Stick with him.

KATE
He doesn't want me along. And I'm not sure I want to go.

HARRY
When he says it, I'll believe it.

KATE
Will you stop being so selfless with my self? Look, maybe you owe him. But you owe me too. And some day I might collect. So just be ready. Got it?

HARRY
Yeah. I got it.

KATE
Okay, let's get down to business. Everything's set for the press conference. Have you told Michael about it yet?

HARRY
I thought I'd break it to him gradually.

KATE
How gradually?

HARRY
Now.

KATE
That's what I thought. Oh well, much ado about nothing.

HARRY
All's well that ends well.

Michael enters with food.

                    MICHAEL
As you like it.

                    HARRY
Maybe we should rehearse?

                    MICHAEL
I know how to eat.

                    KATE
He doesn't do well at press conferences.

                    MICHAEL
Press conferences?

                    HARRY
True. And this will be no ordinary press conference.

                    MICHAEL
We're having a press conference?

                    HARRY
No, we're having a press conference rehearsal. Okay, let's set the stage. Kate, you be the audience.

                    KATE
I can feel it already. A presence.

                    MICHAEL
I don't think I like this. I'm highly suggestible. After I saw "Psycho", I couldn't shower alone for weeks.

                    HARRY
Don't break the mood. Reach out to the other world.

                    MICHAEL
Eighth avenue?

                    HARRY
We're having a séance. You are going to contact the ghost of William Shakespeare.

MICHAEL
Harry, I said I'd write the play and I will. One of these days. But I'm not going to look ridiculous in front of a bunch of reporters. You do it.

HARRY
It won't work that way. Kate, tell him.

KATE
It won't work that way.

HARRY
We aren't going to sell this with a lot of special effects. We'll be austere, serious, scientific. I just want you to close your eyes, sway a little bit, mumble a few unintelligible lines, then wake up and remember nothing. We just have to make them doubt their doubts a little. But it has to be you in there- calm, rational, only slightly wild about the eyes.

MICHAEL
Kate, will you explain to him that this will never work?

KATE
No.

MICHAEL
You see? What do you mean, no?

KATE
I believe it will work.

MICHAEL
You do?

HARRY
You do?

KATE
I do.

MICHAEL
Since when?

HARRY
Yes, since when?

KATE
Since a long time ago. I just forgot. Oh, I don't think anyone is really going to be fooled. But in this business, publicity is money, and this may just generate enough publicity to get it on the boards. Once that happens, who knows?

MICHAEL
You picked a fine time to figure this out.

KATE
The timing has been wrong for all three of us from the very beginning. I wanted you. Harry wanted you. I want Harry. Harry wants me. It's like daytime TV.

MICHAEL
When did all this happen?

HARRY
While you were counting the eggrolls.

MICHAEL
Well, at least it's not sudden or anything. Isn't there supposed to be a period of mourning? At least a moment of silence?

KATE
I had this thought you might be happy. For us.

MICHAEL
Someday I might be.
Dramatically.
Right now I feel like day old bread that's just been tossed in the quick sale bin of life. After all, I do love you.

KATE
How do you know?

HARRY
Yes, how <u>do</u> you know?

MICHAEL
You stay out of this. I know all about love. I've written about it dozen of times.

KATE
I'm not willing to settle for someone who's not willing to settle for me.

MICHAEL
That's not fair.

KATE
You're right. It's not fair—to me.

MICHAEL
Now let me get this straight. After spending the last ten years hating him, you spend five minutes sitting next to him and suddenly decide that it was really love after all.

HARRY
How did you know she was sitting next to me?

MICHAEL
Because. That's how things like this happen.

KATE
Michael, I love you. You know that. But I can't help you anymore. And you can't help me. And he needs all the help he can get.

HARRY
You're right. It is like daytime TV.

MICHAEL
So he needs you and I don't.

KATE
Right.

MICHAEL
Do you need her?

HARRY
I guess so.

MICHAEL
That's quite a declaration of love.

KATE
It's more than I ever got from you.

MICHAEL
At least you could have had the decency to run away together. Forget that, you'd probably want to borrow my car.

KATE
You don't have a car.

MICHAEL
That's a flimsy excuse.

KATE
We don't want to hurt you.

MICHAEL
I see no purpose in staying here any longer.

He starts to leave.

> KATE

Wait.

> HARRY

No. Let him go. We both know he's better off without me. This whole idea was nothing but an old man's fantasy, anyway. How important is that? Anyway, it's finished. I just wish I still had the money.

> KATE

What money?

> MICHAEL

Yes, what money?

> HARRY

No. it's okay. I don't deserve anything from you, regardless of what happens to me.

> KATE

What money?

> HARRY

I'll think of a way out. That's what I'm good at.

> KATE

What money?

> HARRY

We had to have some front money.

> MICHAEL

Harry, where did you get the money?

> HARRY

Oh, hi, Mike, you still here?

> MICHAEL

Yes, I'm still here. Where did you get the money?

HARRY

I—

He mumbles something.

MICHAEL

What?

HARRY

I borrowed it.

KATE

Not from?

Harry nods.

KATE

Oh Harry.

MICHAEL

When did you do this?

HARRY

You didn't really think I went to the library did you?

KATE

This is not good.

HARRY

Things were going so well. We were finally going to do something we could both be proud of, something I could remember while I rocked back and forth on the porch of my little white house back in Kansas.

MICHAEL

Kansas? You've never been past West End Avenue.

HARRY
Whatever. You have to look things in the eye, no matter how devastating they may be. After all, what's the worst that can happen?

MICHAEL
I'm afraid to think about it.

HARRY
I'll be okay. I hear Brazil is nice.

MICHAEL
Harry, pull yourself together. We'll find a way out of this.

HARRY
We will? But how?

MICHAEL
I'll tell you how. I'm going to do this press conference, and when I'm through, they're going to believe in every ghost this side of Stephen King. So what are you waiting for? Let's get this rehearsal started.

HARRY
Okay, if you say so.

KATE
He says so.

MICHAEL
Wait a minute. First things first—I have to save the eggrolls.

Michael exits.

KATE
You are the most evil outrageous manipulative bastard I have ever met.

HARRY
My mother thanks you, my father thanks you, and I thank you.

KATE
That lie goes into your Hall of Fame.

HARRY
I'll have you know every word of that was true. Tomorrow. So you knew all along it was a lie?

KATE
Yes. And so did he.

HARRY
Really. How?

KATE
Your lips were moving. By the way, I'll lend you the money.

HARRY
Beautiful, smart, and rich. I adore you.

Michael enters. Harry and Kate break quickly.

MICHAEL
Okay, we're all set.

HARRY
Not quite.

He unveils some fancy looking equipment, and puts a cheap looking a goldfish bowl on the table.

HARRY
Now.

KATE
Impressive. What is it?

HARRY
This is highly sophisticated scientific equipment.

KATE
Where'd you get it?

HARRY
Jake's Pawn Shop. Cost me fifty bucks.

KATE
What does it do?

HARRY
I haven't the slightest idea. But it looks impressive.

Harry holds up the goldfish bowl, upside down.

KATE
What is that?

HARRY
You can't have a séance without a crystal ball.

KATE
It looks like a goldfish bowl.

He holds it right-side up.

HARRY
This is a goldfish bowl.
He holds it upside down.

HARRY
This is a crystal ball. Okay. Kate, lights.

She goes offstage. They dim.

HARRY
Remember Mike, the key is to upset their expectations. Stay calm, cool, and scientific. No emotion whatsoever. Got it?

MICHAEL
Mystically
I understand.

HARRY
Séance, take one. Ladies and Gentlemen of the fourth estate, may I have your attention please.

I come to bury Caesar, not to praise him.

KATE
Isn't that breaking the news a little soon, Harry?

HARRY
Shaking it off
Anyway... Ladies and Gentlemen, before this night is over, I believe you will feel like me.

KATE
Old.

HARRY
No heckling from the audience, please.

KATE
Sorry.

HARRY
Not long ago, my partner and I took refuge from a roving band of critics who had happened to catch our last show.

KATE
They must have been very quick. Sorry, I'm just trying to make it realistic.

HARRY
That very night, as he hid in terror, he heard a voice whispering to him. The voice was rich and expressive, and spoke:

Thus is his cheek the map of days outworn,
when beauty liv'd and died as flowers do now,
before these bastard signs of fair were born,
and durst inhabit on a living brow,
before ... the golden tresses of the dead...

KATE
What was that?

HARRY
I-I got carried away, I guess.

MICHAEL
This is getting spooky.

HARRY
Relax. Pay no attention to the man behind the curtain. Where was I? Oh yeah. The voice spoke. At first, he thought he was going crazy.

KATE
And he was right.

HARRY
But when the words started flowing from his pen...

MICHAEL
I thought I was at the keyboard.

HARRY
Who are you, Sherlock Holmes? But when the words started flowing from his *keyboard*, he knew he had been visited by none other than the ghost of William Shakespeare. And now, you are called upon to witness the revisitation of this miracle, when my associate again tries to contact the shade of the Bard of Avon.

MICHAEL
It sounds shady, all right.

HARRY
Will you get in the mood, please?

MICHAEL
Sorry. Okay.
Mystically again
I'm in the mood.

HARRY
Ladies and Gentlemen, let us put aside all doubt, all cynicism, and assist Michael as he moves into communion with the spirit world. Okay Mike, you're on. Remember, underplay.

MICHAEL
Okay.
The crystal ball starts to glow.
Hey Harry, that's pretty neat. How does it work?

HARRY
What?

MICHAEL
The crystal ball. How does it glow like that?

HARRY
What are you talking about? There's no glow. I told you, that's a goldfish bowl. I borrowed it from my aunt. Poor fish died so suddenly.

KATE
Harry, did you kill your aunt's goldfish?

HARRY
I prefer to think of it as setting it free in the sewer.

MICHAEL
Still concentrating on the crystal ball.
You mean there's no glow?

                    HARRY
No. You must be seeing a reflection from the lights.

He looks up, sees how dim the lights are, looks at the brightness of the bowl.

                    MICHAEL
          Doubtfully.
That must be it.

                    HARRY
Okay, start again.

                    MICHAEL
Right.

At this point, smoke begins to come from offstage.

                    HARRY
What are you looking at now?

                    MICHAEL
The smoke.

                    HARRY
What smoke?

                    MICHAEL
Don't say what smoke! The smoke. The smoke that is pouring out from wings. I have just one question.

                    KATE
What?

                    MICHAEL
Do we have a fire escape?

                    HARRY
No, Mike, we don't want to do it this big. Remember, underplay.

> KATE

I think he's serious.

> HARRY

He's just playing with us.

> MICHAEL

Playing. That's it. This is some method thing, isn't it? You two cooked this up so I'd know how it feels to be haunted. Well, it worked.

> *He leans on the equipment Harry unveiled. It flares into life, needles jumping, etc.*

> MICHAEL

Harry, turn that stuff off. I don't need any more motivation.

> HARRY

I can't turn it off. It isn't on. It isn't even plugged in.

> MICHAEL

What do you mean it isn't plugged in?

> *He picks up the cord, stares at it.*

Oh.

> *He starts looking around.*

What the hell is going on here?

> VOICEOVER
> *A ghostly, booming voice*

Not Hell, nor Heaven either.

> MICHAEL

Oh, no.

> *A wind begins to blow, and thunder begins to sound, which only Michael notices, naturally.*

> VOICE

Michael? Michael?

MICHAEL
What? What?

HARRY
What?

MICHAEL
Shouting
What do you want?

HARRY
Shouting back
Nothing.
Pause
Why are we shouting?

VOICE
Michael?

MICHAEL
What do you want?

VOICE
You called me.

MICHAEL
Wrong number. It was a mistake. Go away.

VOICE
I am here. I have come for you.

MICHAEL
Thanks for coming. You can go now.

Michael starts looking around for the voice.

KATE
Michael, what are you doing?

MICHAEL
I'm looking for the voice. Come out. Come out, I demand to see you.

The scrim rises upstage. Smoke fills the upstage. And through the smoke, a FIGURE finally appears.

MICHAEL
Stop. I changed my mind. I don't want to see you. Go away. Be gone. Shoo.

The FIGURE steps out of the smoke. He is recognizably WillIAM SHAKESPEARE. All sound and lighting effects stop.

MICHAEL
What light through yonder window breaks?

WILL
Mortal, fear not. Your wish now grants itself.

MICHAEL
It's a dream come true.

He faints

WILL
And our little life is rounded with a sleep.

Blackout

End of Act I

Stephen Evans

Act II Scene 1

Setting: Same

Time: A few moments have passed.

At Rise: Harry is staring at Michael, who is sitting, staring front, mouth open, unable to speak. Will is at this point nowhere to be seen. Kate hangs up her cellphone.

KATE
Okay, it's done—no press conference.

HARRY
Good.
Pause. They watch Michael.
I think it's an improvement

KATE
You're not helping.

HARRY
He never was much of a conversationalist.

KATE
Harry!

HARRY
He could still be useful. As a coat rack, maybe, or a hat stand.

KATE
Harry.

                    HARRY
Have you got a hat?

                    KATE
Stop it. Michael, are you okay?

                    MICHAEL
I...I...

                    HARRY
Too derivative of Beckett, I would say.

                    KATE
What?

                    MICHAEL
I...I...I...

                    HARRY
That's the problem with artists. So often the symbolic becomes merely incomprehensible.

                    MICHAEL
I...I...I...

                    HARRY
Admittedly, there's a certain poetry, but what, finally, does it mean? Could you live your life on the basis of it? This reviewer doesn't think so.

                    MICHAEL
Will.

                    KATE
Will? What do you mean, Will? Will what?

                    MICHAEL
Yum.

                    HARRY
Stand back, he's going to Yum.

KATE

Harry!

MICHAEL
As Michael re-enacts those minutes, ad lib
I...He...first there was...then whoosh...He...fffft...then I plllp.

HARRY
Well, I'm glad we cleared that up.

KATE
Will you be quiet? Michael, what-are-you-trying-to-tell-us?

MICHAEL
He's here.

KATE
He? Who? Harry? You want him to leave? I know I want him to leave.

MICHAEL
No!

KATE
Well do you or don't you?

MICHAEL
No. Will.

HARRY
Oh no, we're back to that again.

Michael gathers himself, pulls them both close, looks around, then whispers

MICHAEL
Shakespeare.

KATE
Yes?

MICHAEL
Here.

KATE
I give up. See what you can do.

HARRY
Look, you're a writer. Write it down.

Michael scribbles furiously and hands the paper to Harry.

HARRY
Reading
The ghost of William Shakespeare was here.

He crumples the paper.

HARRY
To Kate.
Your turn again.

KATE
You're trying to tell us that you saw the ghost of William Shakespeare?
Michael nods his head.
In this room?
Michael again nods his head.
Just now?

MICHAEL
Finally breaking through
It's true.

KATE
Shakespeare.

MICHAEL
Yes. Shakespeare.
to Harry
Just like you've--

> *turning to Kate*

Just like you've always seen him.

> HARRY

We're not the ones seeing things.

> KATE

Leave him alone.

> HARRY

Come on. You don't mean you believe this act? Mike, I know we should have told you about the press conference sooner, but we just finished making the arrangements. Honest.

> MICHAEL

Harry?

> HARRY

Yeah?

> MICHAEL

I saw him.

> HARRY

No.

> MICHAEL

Yes. We've witnessed a miracle. It was Shakespeare.

> KATE

I don't think we should discuss it anymore tonight.

> HARRY

Okay, you've had a busy night. You should get some sleep.

> MICHAEL
> *Standing*

I don't think I could sleep now. I have to prepare my announcement to the world.

HARRY
That's okay. Kate and I will take care of it. You lie down and be spiritual for a while. Kate, why don't you help him lie down and I'll call the d-o-c-t-o-r.

MICHAEL
Scornfully
Do you think Shakespeare would appear to someone who couldn't spell?

HARRY
Sorry, I lost my head.

KATE
Harry's right. You've been under a lot of stress, and you need some rest.

Michael lies down on something funny. Kate covers him with something funnier.

MICHAEL
As long as you believe me.

KATE
I believe you saw something. We'll talk about it tomorrow.

HARRY
Harry stands to the side, watching
There is a tide in the affairs of men,
Which, taken at the flood, leads on to fortune;
Omitted, all the voyage of their life
is bound in shallows, and in miseries.

KATE
He should sleep till morning.

HARRY
He should sleep till morning.

They exit. Michael gets up, pours a drink, sits at his makeshift desk. Then he sees a book.

MICHAEL
The Legend of Sleepy Hollow.
> *He tosses it behind him and picks up the next one.*

A Christmas Carol.
> *He tosses it.*

Hamlet.
> *He tosses it, then thinks better of it. Looking toward heaven*

Sorry!
> *He picks it up. To the book.*

You met a ghost and look what happened to you.
> *He looks up.*

Are you or aren't you, that is the question. Am I better off insane in a simple world where everything unnatural is traced to chemical infraction? Or sane, and sane alone, in a mindless place where every rule of logic has vanished in a rush of photons on an autumn night. Tough choice. If I choose to whimper quietly in my closet for a year, tended to salvation by my friends, then I will. And everything I've seen tonight dissolves into memory. Or, if I choose, then you are real, and the life that I have known is at an end. So. Let it end.

> *Will appears, playing Hamlet, Sr. In a booming, ghostly voice*

WILL
My hour is almost come, when I to sulphurous and tormenting flames must render up myself.
I am thy father's spirit, doomed for a certain term to walk the night and for the day confined to fast in fires, till the foul crimes done in my days of nature are burnt and purged away. But that I am forbid to tell the secrets of my prison house, I could a tale unfold whose lightest word would harrow up thy

soul, freeze thy young blood, make thy two eyes, like stars, start from their spheres-

     MICHAEL
I believe you.

     WILL
   A complete change of tone
You interrupted me. Never interrupt me. You have much to learn.

     MICHAEL
I'm sorry. I guess I don't know how to behave with a...whatever you are.

     WILL
I see.

     MICHAEL
Actually, I'm really glad you're here, because there's a question I want to ask you. Are you really here?

     WILL
   Booming again
You doubt me still?

     MICHAEL
Not that I want you to take it personally. I just thought that as long as you are going to keep popping up, so to speak, we might as well get the social introductions out of the way. So, <u>what</u> are you?

     WILL
I am as you believe.

     MICHAEL
Are you a dream?

     WILL
We are such stuff as dreams are made on.

MICHAEL
Clever. Did you make that up?

WILL
That is the question.

MICHAEL
Quick. You're very quick.

WILL
In truth, I am not.

MICHAEL
I see.
Pause
So. Where do we stand?

WILL
My question exactly.

MICHAEL
You mean you don't know?

WILL
Nothing is clear. I am, or was, Will Shakespeare, born Year of Our Lord 15 and 64, son of John Shakespeare and Mary Arden, late of the King's Men in London.

MICHAEL
Not of an age, but for all time.

WILL
What was that?

MICHAEL
I'm sorry. I was quoting a contemporary of yours, Ben Johnson.

WILL
Beastly man. Never liked him.

MICHAEL
He must have liked you. He wrote the dedication to the first collected version of your plays.

WILL
He did what? That scoundrel had the impudence to write his name on the same page as mine? I'll...
He stops, stunned
How do you know this?

MICHAEL
I know many things about you. You were born and died on the same day, April 23. At age 18, you were married to Anne Hathaway. And in your will, you bequeathed her your second best bed. I always wondered what you meant by that.

WILL
Ah. That was a good bed. Springy, even after all those years in London. Wait. What witchcraft is this? How is it that you know these things?

MICHAEL
Not witchcraft at all. I've studied your life since I was a child. You're taught in every school.

WILL
Taught? You mean, remembered?

MICHAEL
You're an artistic saint, considered the greatest playwright of all time. And, you've been a personal hero of mine for years.

WILL
Remembered. I am remembered. How many years?

MICHAEL
It's the year of your lord 2020.

WILL
Two score decades.
Hardly daring to ask
What of my work? Has anything been saved?

MICHAEL
Nearly all of it, I guess. 37 plays, 154 sonnets, some longer poems.

WILL
37 plays. Did I write 37 plays?

MICHAEL
Some say yes, some no. There are 37 attributed to you.

WILL
37. They are still performed at times?

MICHAEL
More often than any other playwright, except possibly Neil Simon.

WILL
And they are well received? The public mind may now be too refined. Lust and violence may no longer interest them.

MICHAEL
They're still fairly popular.

WILL
The actors, are they well trained? They must be well trained. And the stage-it must be large, but not too large. And the entre-acts. Do they still have bear-baiting? Nothing like a good bear-baiting to keep the audience's interest up.

MICHAEL
I should have tried it with my last show.

WILL
I am remembered. Remarkable.

MICHAEL
Why remarkable? Surely you knew that your work would be preserved.

WILL
I knew it not, not cared. As a living man, I was a desperate soul, and my twisted characters mirrored my own despair. Meaning in life I sought, and finding none, became the voice of darkness. That's why I preferred comedy.

MICHAEL
Really? It's your tragedies that are most famous now.

WILL
Well. They paid the bills.

MICHAEL
I have to ask. Which was your favorite play?

WILL
The best is no doubt is A Midsummer Night's Dream.

MICHAEL
That's my favorite!

WILL
My favorite is probably As You Like It. And anything with Falstaff.

He begins to reminisce.

WILL
Ah Rosalind. She was real, though I never met her in life. I wrote my sonnets for her as well. In her youth she dressed as a man. As she grew older, she grew darker. But still.

MICHAEL
Why have you come back? Why are you here?

WILL
To work. Here can I pour my anguished heart, and so eviscerate a while the dark. For if life was a shadow, death is darker still. I could not work. I could not create. My work was all I had on earth. No longer could I be without.

MICHAEL
You couldn't work?

WILL
Only God creates from nothing, boy. In heaven, there's naught but cold unyielding glory. A darker beauty calls to me. Less lofty, mayhap, but more human. Death. Life. Love. Laughter-there is none in heaven. No laughter. No hope-for hope requires change. Nothing a man can know as beautiful. Heaven is for angels, boy, and saints, and I am neither. So was I sent back. So am I here, returned for one night unto this sphere to find perhaps a trace of hope in beauty, laughter, love in life, enough to last eternity.

MICHAEL
You speak just as I imagine.

WILL
Indeed, exactly as you imagine. The words are from your mind. All that you see and hear of me is framed by your thoughts, so that you may believe and understand. To speak. To pronounce once more this glorious language is a joy I thought forever lost. Even this barbarous version stolen from your mind.

MICHAEL
One night?

WILL
One.

MICHAEL
Why me? What made you choose me?

WILL
I did not choose you, though perhaps you were chosen. This I know: I can appear only to another poet, another artist. Perhaps your spirit was kindred to my own.

MICHAEL
Oh, how I faint when I of you do write,
Knowing a better spirit doth use your name,
And in the praise thereof spends all his might,
To make me tongue-tied, speaking of your fame!

WILL
Sorry.

MICHAEL
What? Wait a minute. Did you do that?

WILL
Yes. My presence draws from weaker minds the words that I have written.

MICHAEL
That's why we were going around quoting Shakespeare, I mean, quoting you, unexpectedly?

WILL
Excitedly
But come, at last, to work. We must be done by morning. For by the light of day, I shall be but a whisper of your dream. Write as I instruct.

MICHAEL
I can't.

WILL
Centuries have I waited for this—you can't?

MICHAEL
No.

WILL
Puzzled
You can't?

MICHAEL
No.

WILL
Upset
You can't?

MICHAEL
No.

WILL
Angry
You can't?

MICHAEL
No.

WILL
Furious
You can't?

MICHAEL
No.

WILL
Calm
I see.
Exploding
Why can't you?

MICHAEL
I can't tell you.

Same pattern again.

WILL
You can't tell me?

MICHAEL
No.

WILL
You can't tell me?

MICHAEL
No.

WILL
You can't tell me?

MICHAEL
No.

WILL
You can't tell me?

MICHAEL
No.

WILL
You can't tell me?

MICHAEL
No.

WILL
I see.
Pause
Why can't you tell me?

MICHAEL
I don't know.

WILL
Starting again
You don't know?

MICHAEL
Please don't start that again.

WILL
What madness is this? This is your dream.

MICHAEL
I know. I'm sorry.

WILL
The miracle shall be lost, and I condemned to silence everlasting.

MICHAEL
I'm sorry. I'd really like to help you. But I just can't.

WILL
We are so alike, my young friend. In every face, we see the hidden thoughts. In every smile, fear. In every curse, desire. Nothing human hides from us, but us. I know your fear. It is the true haunting of your life.

MICHAEL
You know, my Dad called me 'Shakespeare'. He didn't know. I was the first kid in my class to need glasses, and the first on antidepressants. Anyway, by the time I got to college, even you would have had a hard time living up to my expectations. I had no chance at all. I'd written a play. The school agreed to produce it during a festival featuring new works. If it wasn't special enough, then that would be it.

WILL
Quietus with a bare bodkin.

MICHAEL
More likely a bottle of pills. And then I met Harry. Harry was perfect for me, the perfect excuse never to face myself. You know, everyone thinks that he used me. Not true. I used him, and Kate, and anyone else I had to. All that mattered was keeping the illusion that someone else was to blame for what I never did—for what I was afraid I couldn't do. The funny thing is, on the night when that illusion goes berserk, on the night when the real God of the Theater comes to sweep me

off to Broadway paradise, on this night, I can finally grow up and face the truth. I'm not you. I can't ever be you. Or probably anything close. And I'm through trying. I don't want those comparisons anymore. I want to be free. Free to be content with myself. Finally.

    WILL
And what if I told you...

    MICHAEL
Don't. Please.

    WILL
Then I won't.

    MICHAEL
  Pause
Tell me what?

    WILL
Do you think I haven't felt the fear you feel? I have. I feel it even now. You cannot learn how not to fail. The body fails. So does the mind. But you can learn to value your success.

    MICHAEL
What do you mean?

    WILL
I have learned something of eternity. Nothing lasts forever in itself. But what you create, also creates. And this does last, untraceable as the elements after death. So what you create continues to reverberate through life and time, from mind to mind, forever. In truth, what else am I?

    MICHAEL
I wish I could believe you.

    WILL
Believe this. An artist does one simple thing—he arcs the void, as I have reached to you. If you do this, no matter in

how brief or small a way, then you have achieved all a human can. And this is within the grasp of everyone. Your own creation is your own reward.

MICHAEL

I'm not sure how I'll feel in the morning. But now—let's work.

WILL

Lay on, Macduff.

Michael looks at Will expectantly.

Et cetera.

Blackout

End of Act II Scene 1

Act II Scene 2

Setting: The theater.

Time: Morning.

At Rise: Will gazes longingly at the champagne bottle. He sighs.

> WILL

The intensity of sense is what I miss. A good-sherris sack hath a two-fold operation in it. It ascends me into the brain; dries me there all the foolish and dull and crudy vapours which environ it; makes it apprehensive, quick, forgetive, full of nimble fiery and delectable shapes; which, delivered over to the voice, the tongue, which is the birth, becomes excellent wit. The second property of your excellent sherris is, the warming of the blood...

He looks offstage

> WILL

If I had a thousand sons, the first human principle I would teach should be, to forswear thin potations and to addict themselves to sack.

Kate enters. Will's attention immediately turns to her.

> WILL

Age cannot whither her, nor custom stale her infinite variety;

Harry enters, stumbling in, disheveled and unready for

the morning.

WILL
Other women cloy the appetites they feed, but she makes hungry where most she satisfies

Kate and Harry look at each other. It is apparent that their relationship has taken another step. They pause and look at each other.

HARRY
Good morning.

KATE
Good morning.

HARRY
Sleep well?

KATE
Yes. You?

HARRY
Better than I have in about 15 years. Is he up?

KATE
Apparently not. I thought I heard him, though. I wonder how he's doing?

HARRY
Probably better than we are. At least he had a good night's sleep.

KATE
I'm worried about him.

HARRY
That's silly. Last night he was having a little fun with us. We'll all laugh about it this morning over breakfast.

              KATE
I hope so.

   Michael enters, eyes glazed.

              MICHAEL
       To Harry
Good morning.
       To Kate
Good morning.
       To Will
Good morning.
       To all
You want coffee? I made coffee. You need coffee? I need coffee. I'll get coffee.

   Michael exits.

              KATE
He said good morning three times. He said it to you. He said it to me. Then he said it again.

              HARRY
Double vision.

              KATE
Then he'd have said it four times.

              HARRY
One and a half vision.

              KATE
Is that like having half a brain?

              HARRY
He was sleepy. It was a mistake.

              KATE
I guess.

Michael enters, bringing four cups. He gives one to Harry, one to Kate, one to Will.

WILL
Refusing
It's a bit too late for me.

MICHAEL
You mean too early.

WILL
No, too late. By about four centuries.

MICHAEL
Ah, right.

KATE
What?

MICHAEL
What? Did you say something?

KATE
I said what.

MICHAEL
What? What?

KATE
What?

HARRY
This is beginning to sound like Morse code. Did you say something?

MICHAEL
I said what.

HARRY
That's what I want to know. What did you say?

MICHAEL
What.

KATE
Yes, what?

WILL
What, what!

MICHAEL
What? Wait. Whoa.

HARRY
What?

KATE
Wait.

WILL
Well!

MICHAEL
Will!

KATE
Who?

MICHAEL
What? Oh, I'm sorry. Kate, Harry, Will. Will, Kate, Harry.

HARRY
Will we what?

MICHAEL
No. Will.

KATE
Wait. Why-are you drinking two cups of coffee?

MICHAEL
Because it's too late.

KATE
For what?

MICHAEL
For coffee.
> Pause

That doesn't make any sense, does it?
> They stare at him

I'm going to the dressing room to get cleaned up. We'll discuss this later. Oh.

Michael picks up a sheaf of papers and hands it to Harry

MICHAEL
This is for you. I'll be right back.

KATE
That is a seriously disturbed person. He's definitely not the same person he was yesterday.

HARRY
Who is?

KATE
Harry, what if it happened because of us?

HARRY
Us?

KATE
Yes, us. It's been known to happen. I read about it in the New York Post. What if he just couldn't handle it and went over the edge?

WILL
It's possible.

KATE
Maybe he really was in love with me after all. And the way he sees it, we betrayed him. It could make anyone crazy.

WILL
Ah, the plot.

KATE
Think! How would he react?

WILL
He'd cut off their heads.

KATE
He wouldn't get violent.

WILL
Too bad.

KATE
That's not his style. No. He'd dive into the nearest fantasy.

WILL
Fantasy. I like that.

KATE
One that you and I neatly provided.

WILL
We'll need some witches.

KATE
One that would solve all the problems we caused.

WILL
And maybe a few fairies.

KATE
Shakespeare would appear and be his personal savior, to save him from himself, and us.

WILL
That works for me.

KATE
Harry, that's what happened. I'm sure of it. And we're responsible. So it's up to us to do something about it.

HARRY
Like what?

KATE
It's going to mean a sacrifice.

WILL
Human?

KATE
First, we'll have to explain to him that there's nothing between us.

HARRY
There isn't? I could have sworn there was.

KATE
There is. But that's something he can never know.

HARRY
Lying. I can handle that.

KATE
Second, we can't talk about this play, or writing, or Shakespeare. Not for a very long time.

HARRY
What about my idea?

KATE
Harry, do you really think it would have worked?

HARRY
I suppose not. How could he write a play that sounded like Shakespeare?

WILL
There are more things in heaven and earth, Harry, than are dreamt of in your philosophy.

HARRY
Yeah, I guess it's for the best.

Harry looks at the manuscript and reads, gradually getting more and more excited.

KATE
It will be difficult for both of us. But we have to be strong, for his sake. We'll have to go for long walks in the park with him, maybe move to the country. You don't think they'll have to hospitalize him, do you? I couldn't stand to see that. But you know what the hardest part will be? Not letting him see anything between us.

HARRY
looking at the manuscript
I don't believe it.

KATE
It's true. No looking deep into my eyes. No brushing my cheek with your fingers, or smoothing my hair, or running your hand...

HARRY
This is it!

Harry runs to Kate and kisses her wildly.

KATE
No, Harry, we can't. We have to be strong.

He kisses her again.
No, strong, we can't. We have to be Harry.

He drops her suddenly, looking amazed at the manuscript.

HARRY
He did it. He really did it.

KATE
Harry, I cannot deal with two crazy people at once.

HARRY
I always knew he could do it. I never doubted him for a minute. Don't you understand? The play. He wrote it in one night. But that's not the amazing thing. The amazing thing is, it's brilliant.

WILL
Naturally. Or perhaps, supernaturally.

HARRY
I could almost believe Shakespeare came back from the dead to write it.

WILL
There are more things in heaven and earth... wait, I already said that.

KATE
Let me see it.

HARRY
And he did it in one night. I always knew he was a genius. You know what? We're going to be rich. As in having lots and lots of money. Rich!

WILL
Rich!

KATE
No, we're not.

HARRY
We're not?

WILL
We're not?

KATE
No.

HARRY
Why not?

WILL
Yes, why not?

KATE
What are you thinking of?

HARRY
I'm thinking of getting rich. What are you thinking of?

KATE
We have a man in there whose mental welfare is hanging by a thread. This play proves how disturbed he is.

WILL
I beg your pardon.

KATE
Even if it was good, and I don't see how it could be if he wrote it in one night, we can't ever let him see it or hear about it again.

Harry looks at her. Then at the manuscript. Then back at her.

HARRY
But...

KATE
Don't you see? It could be the final shock that does him in, and we may never reach him again.

Harry looks at her. Then at the manuscript. Then back at her.

HARRY
But...

She takes the manuscript.

KATE
Harry, we have to get rid of it. Pretend it never existed.

He takes it back.

HARRY
Now you're the one who is acting crazy. We're talking about a million dollars here. Maybe ten million dollars.

WILL
How much is that in shillings?

KATE
You know, every time I start to feel some hope for you, we always get back to money. Isn't his health and sanity worth more than a few dollars?

HARRY
It isn't the money. Okay, partly it's the money. But don't you see? It's the idea. It could work. Do you know how seldom that happens nowadays? I can't throw that away.

KATE
You have two choices, Harry. You can walk out the door with that manuscript and never come back. Or you can shred it and stay here with me. What's it going to be?

Pause. Will, shocked by the whole turn of events, looks on with horror. Harry looks at Kate, then at the play. He walks quickly to the front door.

KATE
Harry!

HARRY
Just kidding. Never thought I'd turn out to be such a sap.
Harry moves toward the shredder
Do I hafta?

KATE
You hafta.

He starts to move again. Kate stops him

KATE
Harry. Thanks.

HARRY
For you.

Harry reluctantly drops the manuscript in the shredder. Will lets out a bloodcurdling scream. Michael run in.

MICHAEL
What the hell is going on here?

WILL
Horror beyond belief.

KATE
Nothing. What do you mean?

MICHAEL
I heard...

KATE
I told you, nothing. You should get some sleep.

MICHAEL
It's morning.

KATE
Oh. Right. Good morning.

MICHAEL
Sleep well?

Harry	Kate
Yes. No.	No. Yes.

MICHAEL
I see.
He turns to Will
I can't get a straight Answer out of them. How about you?

WILL
The last hundred years were a little restless.

MICHAEL
That's not what I mean.

KATE
Michael, don't.

MICHAEL
Quiet, please. I'm trying to have a conversation.

KATE
Michael, please don't do this to yourself. We aren't worth it.

MICHAEL
I'll get back to that later.

KATE
Michael, there's no one there.

HARRY
Where is there?

MICHAEL
He points to Will
There. And I'm beginning to wish it were true. This is going to be a problem. Wait. I can prove to you that he's real.
Michael looks for the manuscript.
Where'd it go?

WILL
Still in disbelief
They beheaded it.
Michael lets out a scream.
That's what I said.

MICHAEL
You didn't?

WILL
Yes, I did. It sounded just like yours.

HARRY
On a whole different track
No, we didn't. How did you know?

MICHAEL
How could you do it?

KATE
Kicking Harry
How could we do what?

MICHAEL
How could you do... what you did?

KATE
We thought it was the best thing for you.

HARRY
We did?

MICHAEL
Oh. You did. Both of you. Together. My two best friends. And you did it behind my back.

HARRY
Well, we weren't going to do it in front of you.

KATE
Harry, shut up. It was an accident.

HARRY
It was?

MICHAEL
How could it be an accident?

KATE
To Harry
I don't think you should say anymore.

MICHAEL
Just tell me it isn't true.

HARRY
I can't. I have to be honest.

KATE
Since when?

HARRY
Kate and I slept together last night.

MICHAEL
I knew that.

HARRY
I know it's a shock.

KATE
You knew that?

HARRY
I told you he knew. How'd you know?

MICHAEL
I don't care about that. I'm talking about something serious.

KATE
And my sleeping with Harry isn't? You are crazy.

MICHAEL
Look, whatever you two did last night is okay with me. I'm all for it. I was just pretending to be upset because I didn't want you to think I didn't care.

KATE
What?

MICHAEL
I mean I thought we needed to have a serious discussion about the future of our relationship.

KATE
I'll tell you what your future is…

Harry holds her back

MICHAEL
Stop trying to change the subject. I want to know why you beheaded, I mean shredded, my manuscript.

HARRY
How did you know we shredded it? We never said that.

MICHAEL
I have friends in high places.

HARRY
It's getting weird again.

MICHAEL
I want to know why you shredded my play. It was the answer to everything. For all of us.

KATE
All four of us?

MICHAEL
As a matter of fact, yes.

KATE
Michael, sit down here. You're right. We have to talk.
Michael sits next to her.
I know that what has happened, what we've done, has hurt you.
Michael starts to say something.
Please don't deny it.
He tries again.
Please. Let me finish. I know that we've hurt you. And I know that hurt has caused you to seek refuge in this fantasy. I'm not going to argue with you. I just want you to know that what happened between Harry and me last night is over, and it will never happen again. From now on, I'm going to dedicate my life to making you well.

We did shred your play, I admit it. And I know it was a terrible thing to do. But we had no choice. As long as it was around, you'd never let go of your fantasy world. You'll write other plays, better ones, once you come back to the real world. I know you can't do it all at once. But someday, you will. And I'll be with you.

HARRY
And I won't.

MICHAEL
What?

HARRY
I've hurt you enough, kid. I've taken everything you had to give, until all that's left is a deluded husk of a man.

MICHAEL
Who are you calling a husk?

HARRY
I've taken the wheat and thrown the chaff away into the gutter and watched it wash down the wrong side of the street, mixing with the dirt and the grime and the refuse until it becomes a filthy worthless inhuman...

MICHAEL
I get the picture.

HARRY
Sorry. Anyway, I'm leaving. You'll both be better off without me around to screw things up.

MICHAEL
Time out here. This isn't what I planned. Just let me think for a minute.

He moves away.

WILL
Plot problems? I hate those.

MICHAEL
I don't get it. This could have been the greatest night of my life. I had everything I ever wanted. I met William Shakespeare. I wrote the play of my dreams. I was inches away from fame, fortune, American Express commercials.

MICHAEL
And now everything has fallen apart. Kate is leaving Harry for me. Harry is leaving, period. And the play is gone. My finest work is now ticker tape. My life is over.

WILL
Dramatic, but unconvincing.

MICHAEL
What do you mean?

WILL
I know that you have a copy of the play on your clever device. Why pretend otherwise? I wrote this scene, remember? Henry IV, Part 2. Prince Hal rids himself of the loyal Falstaff, leaves the friends who supported him in his youth, ascends to the crown and lives gloriously ever after as King Henry V. Falstaff of course dies of loneliness and cruelty, but such is the price of kingship.

MICHAEL
That can't be me.

WILL
Fate has taken reign and delivered your desires.

MICHAEL
I wouldn't do that.

WILL
Make not the mistakes I made!

MICHAEL
Would I? I mean, without them, it means nothing. I need them. I need them both. I can't believe I'm saying this. Great. Thank you for pointing out how much I need them just when I'm about to lose them both. Harry's still going to leave. Kate still thinks I'm crazy. And she'll go on burning every copy of the play I can put together, until she's convinced otherwise.

WILL
That is a problem.

MICHAEL
There's only one solution. They have to believe in you.

WILL
It seems the only answer.

MICHAEL
Great.

WILL
Unfortunately it's impossible.

MICHAEL
It can't be impossible. It happened to me. There must be some way for them to see you, too.

WILL
You and I are artists. Our spirits are in harmony. That is why you see, and why they cannot.

MICHAEL
I don't understand.

WILL
Your heart and mine found meaning in creation, the life of beauty, the service of the art. But what answer is true for every man? On either side of death, I know of none. Each must choose his own, or else have none. If their choice be not the match and complement to mine, some other spirit may answer. But I may not.

MICHAEL
I believe you are the truth. And I believe they need to share that truth. And I can't believe that something so real and meaningful to me cannot touch them as well.

> *All this time, Harry and Kate have observed this conversation, though to them it appears Michael is talking to the air. Kate breaks down, and Harry tries to*

comfort her, though he is greatly pained himself. Michael goes to Harry and Kate.

MICHAEL
Look. Look at these two people.

KATE
Michael, don't do this.

MICHAEL
Are you saying you have nothing to give to them? I don't believe it. These are the people you were writing for all along. You didn't write for the scholars who count up the number of times you wrote the word 'moon'. Or the actors who stammer out your speeches or the directors who twist your plays in the name of creativity. You wrote for people just like them. Maybe they are ordinary. I mean, God knows, Harry's a liar, a cheat, and a thief, and that's just for starters.

HARRY
That's not fair. If I say I'm not a cheat, that makes me a liar.

MICHAEL
And Kate. You have always known the truth about us. You have dedicated your life to two men who have dedicated their lives to hurting you. Here we are, the saint, the clown, and the villain, three perfect players come to life. What would you have us do, master playwright? I'll tell you this. If you cannot reach their hearts, you'll have none of mine.

WILL
So you think I need motivation, do you? Some incentive to shake four hundred years of rust?

MICHAEL
I'm sorry. I should realize I can't manipulate you. Habit, I guess. The real truth is, I needed you but didn't deserve you. They need you, and do.

WILL
Vision is birth. It requires pain. Their need is great, that is plain enough. But I see no hope.

Will begins to walk around as if studying them. He stops at Harry. Harry follows Michael's eyes following Will and begins to get nervous.

MICHAEL
Try.

HARRY
Stop looking at what I'm not seeing.

WILL
Very well. First we must make them doubt their doubts. We must create the question in their minds. I believe I know a way.

MICHAEL
Go ahead.

Will gestures to Harry.

HARRY
Mike, this is ridiculous.
Harry turns to Kate
Will you please tell him-

The brain of this foolish-compounded clay, man,
is not able to invent anything that tends to laughter,
more than I invent or is invented on me:

I am not only witty in myself, but the cause that wit is in other men.

          KATE

How did you-

      Will gestures to Harry.

Pale as his shirt, his knees knocking each other;
and with a look so piteous in purport
as if he had been loosed out of Hell
to speak of horrors, he comes before me.

         MICHAEL

Mad for thy love?

          KATE

My Lord, I do not know;
But truly I do fear it.

Hypnosis. Or something, I don't know. I won't believe in ghosts.

         HARRY

I will.

          WILL

Yes. The potential for alignment now exists. The doubt and the desire are there. But that is not enough.

         HARRY

I think I see something.

          WILL

Only another creative mind can make the final link.

         HARRY

I hear something too.

          WILL

Only an artist's soul can apprehend my visage.

HARRY
It's him!

WILL
Silence! He interrupts more than you.

HARRY
Sorry.

Will and Michael realize that Harry can now see and hear Will.

MICHAEL
We may have to revise your theory.

WILL
It can't be. Only an artist. I'm sure.

HARRY
What's he upset about?

MICHAEL
You're not supposed to be able to see him. You're not an artist.

HARRY
Some people consider me an artist.

MICHAEL
Who?

HARRY
'Fingers' Morgan. 'Loose Lips' Louie...

MICHAEL
We're not talking about con artists.

WILL
Yes, we are.

HARRY
You know 'Loose Lips'?

WILL
There are many kinds of artists, are there not? Some work in stone, some sound, some light. And some there are that only work in dreams. Often they fail, as dreams are wont to do. But for all that, their craft is true and worthy of the name of art. The dreamer reads the mind of God. Here is no master of the craft. But the dream that we now live was born in the laughter of your heart. As your creation, we dream, and we endure.

HARRY
I feel like I've lived my whole life in Kansas, and I just jumped over the rainbow.

All three turn to look expectantly at Kate.

MICHAEL
To Will
You're two for two. Care to try for three?

KATE
You're both crazy and I'm leaving.

HARRY AND MICHAEL
No!

HARRY
Kate, you have to trust me on this. One last time. All or nothing.

Kate turns away.

KATE
I don't know what to believe anymore. Maybe Shakespeare's ghost is zooming around the room at this very minute. It

doesn't matter. Don't you understand? I'm a normal person. I need normal things. I don't need to write great plays or make up fancy schemes. I just need someone to love. And someone to love me. And I'm not even sure anymore that they need to be the same person. I'll take what I can get. But I can't get it here.

Will laughs.

WILL

I understand. Fear not. We shall reach her. For hers is the noblest art of all, the art that forms in flesh and shapes our souls. This also did I miss on earth. In binding flesh, we bound the universe. What we create cannot compare with this: life gets love, so love gets life. And the life that's now within grows in that love.

So long as men can breathe, or eyes can see,

So long lives this, and this gives life to thee.

Kate stays very still, as if listening. Will whispers something to her. Slowly, she turns to look at Will, and smiles.

KATE

Thank you.

HARRY

What did he say?

KATE

This were to be new made when thou art old,
And see thy blood warm when thou feel'st it cold.

WILL
Walking to the laptop

Well put. 'Tis why I was sent back. I had to see that I have moved beyond. 'Twas you who knew. Some other work there is that beckons. A different beauty calls, an eternity to create. That is heaven.

Will passes his hand over the laptop

Alas, my friends, The gloworm shows the matins to be near, and 'gins to pale his ineffectual fire. Adieu. Adieu. Hamlet, remember me.

MICHAEL
It waves me still. Go on, I'll follow thee.

WILL
No! You are released to your own voice, as I am to mine. You will know what to say.

MICHAEL
Do you hafta?

WILL
I hafta.

MICHAEL
Go on. I'll follow thee.

KATE
How can we ever thank you?

WILL
The chance of meeting you has paid all debt.

HARRY
If you're ever in the market for a producer...

WILL
Yes?

HARRY
I'll make a few calls.

Will moves to Michael.

MICHAEL
Is this the end?

WILL
In other space and time, perhaps we may yet meet again.
> *Will walks upstage. The smoke begins to rise. He turns.*

...Now I want Spirits to enforce, art to enchant: And my ending is despair, Unless I be relieved by prayer, Which pierces so that it assaults Mercy itself and frees all faults. As you from crimes would pardon'd be, Let your indulgence set me free.

Will disappears.

HARRY
I've always admired a good exuent.

KATE
That's an art you'll have to forget.

MICHAEL
I'll drink to that.

They break out the champagne.

KATE
> *Kate starts to drink, but changes her mind*

No, I'd better not.
> *Michael runs to the laptop.*

Michael, what are you doing?

MICHAEL
I have to see if it's still there.

KATE
What?

MICHAEL
The play.

HARRY
Please, please, please tell me it is.

Michael stops, puzzled.

MICHAEL
It's gone.

HARRY
Pushing lots of buttons
You must be pushing the wrong buttons.

MICHAEL
No. He said it. I am released to my own voice.

HARRY
Oh. Too bad. But never mind that. I've got an idea that's even better.

KATE
No!

HARRY
Kate, this is different. You'll love this one. It's about these two guys who try this scam about writing a play by Shakespeare...

MICHAEL
Shaking his head
It'll never work.

KATE
Sorry, you'll be much too busy...

HARRY
Why?

                    KATE
Taking care of our child...

                    HARRY
Who?

                    KATE
At our beach house in Malibu...

                    HARRY
Where?

                    KATE
After I take that studio job...

                    HARRY
What?

                    KATE
While you retire and write your memoirs.

                    HARRY
When?

                    KATE
Which ought to be worth a hefty advance...

                    HARRY
                Eyes starting to glow
How?

                    KATE
If you have the right agent. And I'd say that you do.

                    HARRY
You may have something there.

                    KATE
I'd say that I do.

                    HARRY
But how...

Pause
Aren't you going to interrupt me?

KATE
Harry, I would never interrupt you...

HARRY
But...

KATE
As long as I've finished speaking. Equal time?

HARRY
We'll negotiate.

KATE
I'll look forward to it. Now as you were saying...

HARRY
But how...
Cautious
about Michael?

KATE
Yes, how about it, Michael? Harry's memoirs. Ever thought of being a ghost writer?

MICHAEL
It's what I live for.
To the Audience
Ours be your patience then, and yours our parts,
Your gentle hands lend us, and take our hearts.

He looks up
All's Well.

STEPHEN EVANS

Blackout

The End

Playwright's Note

The lines in **boldface** are quotations from Shakespeare. They are distinguished from other Shakespearean quotes in the play in that the characters are compelled to say them.

The lines may be accompanied by a lighting change to indicate a supernatural effect. The lines should be spoken in natural rhythms and inflections, and should blend with the character's natural speech. Only after they have said the lines should the characters realize they have uttered something strange

STEPHEN EVANS

Acknowledgements

The Ghost Writer was first produced in 1990 by the Annapolis Theater Project in Annapolis, MD. It was produced again in 1991 by the Guerilla Theater in Kansas City, Kansas, and again in 2013 by Theater 11 in Annapolis, MD.

STEPHEN EVANS

Monuments

A Play in One Act

STEPHEN EVANS

"On this green bank, by this soft stream,
We set today a votive stone;
That memory may their deed redeem,
When, like our sires, our sons are gone.

        Ralph Waldo Emerson

        Concord Hymn

STEPHEN EVANS

For those who remember those who don't.

Cast of Characters

WALDO   Ralph Waldo Emerson.

NELLY   Emerson's Daughter Ellen, referred to as Nelly to avoid confusion.

ELLEN   Emerson's first wife.

LIDIAN   Emerson's second wife.

HENRY   Henry David Thoreau.

LOUISA   Louisa May Alcott.

Scene

A boat on the Nile River.

Time

1873.

STEPHEN EVANS

Act I Scene 1

Setting: Emerson's cabin. Downstage right is Emerson's desk, a small round table really, covered with books, papers, writing paraphernalia, and an oil lamp. A chair behind is behind the table, so the actor faces the audience. Up left is a doorway. Downstage from that is a window of sorts. Across the stage there is a sofa or bench, with assorted chairs around.

At Rise: Waldo is at his desk. He is struggling to light an oil lamp.

WALDO
Let there be light.

NELLY (OFFSTAGE)
Papa, you should come out on deck. You can see the pyramids.

WALDO
I imagine they will last until the return trip.

Nelly laughs, entering through the door.

NELLY
What are you working on, Papa?

WALDO
Genesis.

She laughs.

NELLY
Can you be more specific?

WALDO
Chapter 1, verse 3.

He fiddles with the lamp.

NELLY
Are you writing about it?

WALDO
No, I am re-enacting it.

He fiddles some more, without success, then throws up his hands.

WALDO
Let there be light!

She moves to the desk, places the book down on the desk, and lights the lamp for him.

NELLY
There. Now you can call the light day.

WALDO
Squinting
I would call this dim not day.

NELLY
And set about dividing the darkness from the light.

WALDO
Wishful thinking, daughter.

NELLY
As you have always done, Papa.

She kisses his forehead and looks at the desk.

NELLY
What are you working on today instead of talking a stroll on deck with your devoted daughter?

WALDO
Plutarch's Morals. I wish Henry were here. He knew the Greeks so much better than I.

Nelly is struck with sadness.

NELLY
He is gone, Papa. Henry Thoreau died ten years ago.

Waldo stops, confused, then struggles to remember, accepts, then tries to cover his struggle. Nelly waits patiently for his mind to catch up.

WALDO
Then I don't wish he were here. He would be annoyed with me for disturbing his lecture to the Almighty.

Nelly laughs, but the sadness shows through.

NELLY
You are a wise man.

Waldo, all too aware of his decline, smiles.

WALDO
So everyone tells me.

NELLY
Do you doubt it, O Sage of Concord?

WALDO
Among many things.

Nelly tries to change the subject.

NELLY
I thought Plutarch was a Roman.

WALDO
No. He was a citizen of the Empire, but he was Greek by birth, and by thought.

NELLY
Plutarch was one of my favorites as a child. When you were away on your lecture tours, I would sneak into your study and read him.

WALDO
You were a precocious child. I credit your mother with that. I was away so often. Did you read the Lives?

NELLY
No. Too stuffy, too many wars. I liked the Morals actually. Is this Professor Goodwin's translation?

WALDO
Yes. I am to write the introduction and must have it ready soon.

Again, the sadness hits her. She gathers herself, crosses back to the desk, and lays her hand on his shoulder with great tenderness.

NELLY
That is already done, Papa.

She turns to the front of the book.

NELLY
Reading
With an introduction by Ralph Waldo Emerson.

Waldo looks at the book, confused. He turns a few pages. Then turns a few back, always the familiar struggle to comprehend, catch up with the world.

WALDO
It is done.
> *Another pause.*

Wonderful!
> *He relaxes.*

Oh I am quite relieved. I was dreading the labor. The words do not. Flow. As easily these days.
> *He shakes it off, returning to a familiar quotation to explain the lapse.*

But who cares? As soon as we walk out of doors, Nature transcends all poets so far, that a little more or less skill in whistling is of no account.[1]

Nelly understands, glances outside, then at him, and takes charge, as she has so often done and will continue to do for the rest of his life.

NELLY
Papa, come out of this stuffy cabin and we'll find chairs in the sun and watch the ages float past us.

He smiles at her, grateful for her concern and her care.

The smile fades.

---
[1] From a letter to Caroline Sturgis, Oct. 23, 1857

He looks around the cabin, again deep in confusion.

WALDO
This is a boat.

NELLY
Patiently
Yes, Papa.

Waldo tries to solve the puzzle.

WALDO
Not on the ocean.

NELLY
No.

WALDO
A river?

NELLY
Yes.

WALDO
A river.

NELLY
Yes.

He looks out the window.

WALDO
The Concord?

NELLY
No.

WALDO
No. Too large. Nor the Charles either.

NELLY

Gently

It is the Nile.

Pause.

WALDO

The Nile?

NELLY

We are in Egypt, Papa. We are sailing down the Nile on a boat named the Aurora. Remember how shocked we were at the price? Eight dollars a day.

Slowly it dawns and he catches up.

WALDO

Yes. I remember now. Can we afford such extravagance?

She puts a hand on his shoulder.

NELLY

We can. Remember the fire?

WALDO

The fire. Yes! The fire.

NELLY

The fire burned our house.

WALDO

Yes. Yes. Our poor home.

NELLY

Then your friends and so many admirers raised the money to send us on this trip while it is restored.

He is lost in thought for a moment. Then he notices the book in front of him and turns back to it, something solid he understands.

WALDO
According to Plutarch, the Egyptians invented horticulture.

NELLY
And slavery.

WALDO
The Egyptians did not invent slavery. They merely perfected it.

NELLY
That I thought was an American accomplishment.

WALDO
Now, now. Mr. Lincoln fixed all that.

NELLY[2]
Papa, surely you don't think—
She sees him smiling.
Yes, you know me well.

Nelly picks up the volume, begins flipping pages.

NELLY
I loved these stories. Especially...
She finds the one she wants
Isis and Osiris. I used to read this one over and over.

---

[2] Ellen, her mother Lidian, Henry Thoreau, and about half of Concord were staunch abolitionists and initially supporters of John Brown. Emerson, though not as personally passionate, sometimes lent his famous name to the cause.

                    WALDO
That is hardly a story for children!

                    NELLY[3]
Exactly why I loved it! It is the oldest love story in the world. Osiris was entombed by Typhon and thrown into the sea and Isis searched all over the world for him and opened the coffin and took out the body and laid her cheek against his and then Typhon found the body and cut it up into pieces and threw it into the Nile and Isis searched the river and found every piece except—

                    WALDO
Yes. Yes. I know the story.

                    NELLY
For a young girl, it was scandalous. And very romantic.

Waldo gazes out the window.

                    WALDO
It happened here, if it happened. Thousands of years ago. The tomb of Osiris is on the island of—

                    NELLY
Philae[4].

                    WALDO
Philae, which lies...

                    NELLY
Not far ahead of us.

---

[3] Ellen never married, living in her father's house for the rest of her life, an adoring aunt to her sibling's children.
[4] Pronounced Fi-Lee

Philae reminds Waldo of something. He starts to drift away into memory.

WALDO
I have wanted to see Philae for many years.

NELLY
The captain tells me that the Wards are there, with Clover Adams[5].

WALDO
Many many years.

NELLY
I arranged transportation for us on Philae so we may join them straightaway.

He pauses, then comes back. He turns to Nelly, takes her hands, and looks at her approvingly.

WALDO
You remind me of your mother, Ellen.

She brushes the white hair away from his forehead.

NELLY
I was named for her, Papa. But your first wife Ellen was not my mother.

He laughs.

---

[5] Wife of Henry Adams and the inspiration for some of Henry James characters.

WALDO
I am forgetful now I know. But that I have not forgotten. Your mother Lidian is the best woman, the best wife. She deserves...she deserves...you. You should be home helping her restore our home, not running away to foreign lands with your old Papa.

Waldo stares at his hands.

NELLY
Don't think of that now. There will be time enough for setting things right when we return home. If mother and Edith have not already done so.

WALDO
If anyone can, it is...Lidian. She is...the best woman, the best wife.

NELLY
Papa?

WALDO
Yes?

NELLY
I often wonder...

WALDO
As do I. In the blood I suppose. The wandering wondering Emersons.

NELLY
I often wonder, I was saying.

WALDO
If you are saying, you might as well say.

NELLY
I often wonder how you managed to convince Mother to name me after your first wife. And not just one name. She was Ellen Tucker Emerson. I am Ellen Tucker Emerson.

WALDO
You have wondered that?

NELLY
Can you blame me?

WALDO
I suppose not. Best ask your mother.

NELLY
I have. She said to ask you.

WALDO
Did she?

NELLY
She did. I think she was curious what your answer would be.

WALDO
So am I.

NELLY
I should like to know. If you remember.

WALDO
While I remember, you mean.

NELLY
You must have been quite persuasive. Even for Ralph Waldo Emerson.

WALDO

I suppose it was my idea. Back then I had that much audacity, and that little understanding of women. But your mother must have agreed.

NELLY

Apparently. But why?

WALDO

My first wife and I were married not even two years before she died, and she was ill with the consumption so much of that. I think we knew before we married.

NELLY

Knew what?

WALDO

That we had not much time.

He is lost in thought again. Then, again, returns to the book.

WALDO

I wish Henry were here. He knew the Greeks so much better than I.

Nelly sighs.

NELLY

I shall be on deck, Papa, riddling the sphinx. Join me.

Nelly exits.

WALDO

One monument to another, eh?

He continues to turn pages, then finally finds what he wants.

WALDO

Reading

With an introduction by Ralph Waldo Emerson.

He turns a few pages.

WALDO

Reading

Plutarch's popularity will return in rapid cycles. If over-read in this decade, so that his anecdotes and opinions become commonplace, and to-day's novelties are sought for variety, his sterling values will presently recall the eye and thought of the best minds, and his books will be reprinted and read anew by coming generations. And thus Plutarch will be perpetually rediscovered from time to time as long as books last.[6]

He closes the book.

WALDO

It is finished. I didn't know. I didn't remember. But how can one know what has been forgotten? Is there some sign? An empty space where memories used to be? Like a piece missing from a puzzle?

He sighs.

WALDO

I should like to know what I don't know. Even if that is the only thing I can know.

---

[6] *Plutarch's Morals, with an Introduction by Ralph Waldo Emerson*

He opens the book again, turns the pages more and more rapidly, almost desperately, then finally finds what he wants.

WALDO
Reading
And in the first place where she could take rest, and found herself to be now at liberty and alone, she opened the ark, and laid her cheeks upon the cheeks of Osiris, and embraced him and wept bitterly[7].

ELLEN (O.S.)
We knew.

This voice. He can almost remember it.

WALDO
We knew?

ELLEN (O.S.)
That we had not much time.

More familiar.

WALDO
Did we?

ELLEN O.S.
We spoke of it.

Waldo closes the book.

WALDO
I do not believe in the immortality of the individual soul.

---

[7] *Of Isis and Osiris*, Plutarch's Morals

                            ELLEN O.S.
Since when?

> *He stands. The light grows around him.*

                            WALDO
Since I lost you.

> *He turns. Ellen is revealed, wearing her funeral dress.
> Her face is covered by a veil.*

                            ELLEN
You never lost me.

                            WALDO
I couldn't find you.

                            ELLEN
It's not the same.

                            WALDO
Nothing is.

                            ELLEN
Nothing is.

> *Ellen crosses down into the light.*

                            ELLEN
Anyway I'm not a ghost or a spirit or a lost soul. I'm a memory.

                            WALDO
Well then I suppose you can stay. There is plenty of room. Most of the other memories have left. And they took yesterday with them.

ELLEN
You haven't forgotten me, have you, Waldo? Have you forgotten your Ellinelli? Your Lady Frolick? Lady Pensero? Have you forgotten your queen, my king?

WALDO
Facts fade. Feelings remain.

ELLEN
You can't have forgotten everything. Else I would not be here.

WALDO
How can one know?

ELLEN
A puzzle. But then you like puzzles.

WALDO
Do I?

ELLEN
I hope so. I am one.

She laughs. He smiles at the sound.

WALDO
That is familiar.

ELLEN
Memories are like some old aunt who goes in and out of the house, and occasionally recites anecdotes of old times and persons which I recognize as having heard before, and she being gone again I search in vain for any trace.[8]

---

[8] *Essay on Memory*, Emerson

WALDO
That sounds like something I wrote.

ELLEN
You did. About 15 years ago.

WALDO
If you are a memory, how is it that you know something I wrote years after.

ELLEN
Memories don't abide alone. We coexist.

WALDO
Really?

ELLEN
Oh yes. We speak to one another often.

WALDO
Memories speak to memories. That puts Homer in a different light.[9]

Ellen laughs

ELLEN
Speak, Memory—Of the cunning hero.

WALDO
The wanderer, blown off course time and again.

---

[9] The beginning of the Odyssey.

ELLEN
Well, think of it. What else is there to do but speak to each other? Especially when you spend so little time with us. Such a busy important man, always travelling around giving speeches.

WALDO
Lectures, not speeches. Politicians give speeches.

She sticks her tongue out at him through the veil, laughs, spinning away, her white dress flowing around her. She stops, then turns slyly back to Waldo.

ELLEN
In fact, Lidian and I have spoken.

WALDO
Pardon?

ELLEN
Lidian. Your second wife. You member her, don't you?

WALDO
Oh yes.

ELLEN
I thought so. Lidian and I have had long conversations.

WALDO
About me?

ELLEN
Oh yes!

WALDO
On no!

ELLEN

Poor Waldo.

WALDO

That I remember. You called me that often.

ELLEN

Dear Waldo.

WALDO

Dear Waldo. I remember that too. No one else has ever called me that. Lidian calls me Mr. Emerson.

ELLEN

Sweet Waldo.

WALDO

I know she has never called me that. Not in my hearing anyway.

ELLEN

Never can love make consciousness and ascription equal in force. There will be the same gulf between every me and thee, as between the original and the picture.

Lidian enters, carrying a stack of books, on top of which is a pie.

LIDIAN

I was not your first love. That was her. Beautiful and dead at twenty. What mature woman could compete with that? We named our eldest daughter after her. Ellen. You see I knew. Ellen would be my child and not his wife in time. Though I did not then comprehend how long In Time could be when one is married. Now I know. Now I have learned In Time. My name you changed. From Lydia to Lidian. My Asia as well. You needed something grander I suppose. Jackson or

Emerson, I knew who I was. And Mrs. Emerson when you were cross. But a sweet man, all in all, even sweeter as you faded late. Our Waldo, we lost. Only five years old. Broke your heart, and mine. After Waldo nothing was the same. Dear Henry too. Nothing more to say. And the house. My old house, burned away. We sent you off. I was the one to try to put our seasons back in place. You went with Ellen. Edith came to me. If that was not our life, then I don't know. You mourned your books. I mourned, what did I mourn? A cushion I had mended just that day. A hat that I had always meant to wear. A pie left cooling on the windowsill. Did I mourn there was no more to mourn? No. My accumulations were not singed.

WALDO

Ah you still ask me for that unwritten letter always due, it seems, always unwritten, from year to year, by me to you, dear Lidian...a photometer cannot be a stove. It must content you for the time, that I truly acknowledge a poverty of nature, & have really no proud defence at all to set up, but ill-health, puniness, and Stygian limitation. Is not the wife too always the complement of the man's imperfections, and mainly of those half men the clerks? Besides am I not , O best Lidian, a most foolish affectionate goodman & papa, with a weak side toward apples & sugar and all domesticities, when I am once in Concord? Answer me that. Well I will come again shortly and behave the best I can. Only I foresee plainly that the trick of solitariness never never can leave me.[10]

Lidian grimaces, starts to exit.

---

[10] Letter to Lidian 1848.

ELLEN

She does call you poor Mr. Emerson, if that is any consolation.

He turns back to Ellen.

ELLEN

You love her.

Lidian stops but does not turn back.

WALDO

It is, imprecise, to use the same word for what I felt for you, and what I feel for her. But it is the only word we are given. Even Shakespeare never found another. So I suppose we must make the best of it.

LIDIAN

We must make the best of it.

The light fades on Lidian, then on Ellen.

ELLEN

But this dream of love, though beautiful, is only one scene in our play. In the procession of the soul from within outward, it enlarges its circles ever, like the pebble thrown into the pond, or the light proceeding from an orb.[11]

The light fades on on Ellen.

HENRY

Let there be light.

---

[11] *Essay on Love*, Emerson

Waldo turns. Light comes up on Henry at the desk. He is lighting the lamp.

WALDO
Hello, Henry. How are the beans?

HENRY
Welcome, Mr. Emerson. Beans?

WALDO
Yes, Henry. Mrs. Emerson has sent me for some beans.

Pause.

HENRY
Beans.

WALDO
Beans?

Henry nods.

Waldo smiles. This is a game they play, a contest, but beneath the tension between them is only barely hidden.

Waldo thinks.

WALDO
Pounding beans is good to the end of pounding empires one of these days; but if, at the end of years, it is still only beans![12]

HENRY
Ha!

Henry picks up a piece of paper and reads.

---

[12] Emerson. *Eulogy of Thoreau*

HENRY

The same sun which ripens my beans illumines at once a system of earths like ours.[13]

Waldo nods.

WALDO

You.

Henry nods.

WALDO

Is that new?

HENRY

It is. A book I think. Maybe a lecture. But I think it's a book.

WALDO

About?

HENRY

Me I suppose.

WALDO

You?

HENRY

Yes.

WALDO

You're writing about you?

HENRY

Franklin did it. Rousseau did it.

---

[13] Thoreau, *Walden*

WALDO

Of course, Henry. Of course.

HENRY

Even you have done it, Mr. Emerson.

WALDO

When?

HENRY

In your essay Experience. You wrote about your child. About Waldo. How you felt. When he. Became ill. [14]

WALDO

Yes. Yes. But. That was to illustrate a point. I wasn't writing about myself.

HENRY

I am doing the same. Just on a slightly larger scale.

WALDO

What point are you illustrating?

HENRY

I'm not sure yet.

WALDO

I see.

HENRY

It's a work in progress.

WALDO

Aren't they all?

---

[14] Emerson's son Waldo died of scarlet fever at age five.

HENRY
It's about. My time here.

WALDO
DaVinci said that art is never finished.

HENRY
What I have learned.

WALDO
Art may never be finished, but that cannot be said for artists.

HENRY
What I have—experienced.

WALDO
L'arte non è mai finita.

HENRY
What?

WALDO
DaVinci. That's what he said. I thought you knew Italian, Henry.

HENRY
Italian? A bit. I'm better at French. Latin. Spanish. German. Greek.

WALDO
And your English is coming along well too.

HENRY
Is it? Praise from Ralph Waldo Emerson himself. What more could one ask?

WALDO
You have so much promise Henry. I don't want you to waste it.

Henry holds up a sheaf of papers.

HENRY
I am transforming my journal into a book.

Waldo smiles.

WALDO
Now where did you learn to do that?

HENRY
I wonder.

Henry puts down the papers, looks around the cabin.

HENRY
I'm thinking of calling it Life in the Woods.

WALDO
These are hardly the woods, Henry.

Henry smiles.

HENRY
It is a domestic wilderness.

WALDO
Henry, you know I dislike it when you do that. It is a rhetorical trick of which you are much too fond.

Henry smiles more broadly.

HENRY
I know.

Now Waldo smiles.

WALDO
Ha. Anyway, you're a mile from the town common.

Henry pauses. Back to the game.

HENRY
Common.

Waldo takes his time. Then.

WALDO
Nothing astonishes men so much as common sense and plain dealing.[15]

Henry picks up his sheath of papers again.

HENRY
If one advances confidently in the direction of his dreams, and endeavors to live the life which he has imagined, he will meet with a success unexpected in common hours.[16]

They pause.

WALDO
You again.

HENRY
Yours was good though.

WALDO
Thank you. I'll have to try and remember it.

---

[15] Emerson, *Art*
[16] Thoreau, *Walden*

Waldo takes the sheath of papers from Henry.

He peruses them.

Mumbling.

Nodding.

Scowling.

Henry gets nervous.

> HENRY
> The town common is a mile and three quarters.

> WALDO
> *Not looking up*
> You are the surveyor. I bow to your superior knowledge.
> *Now he looks up.*
> As to distance.

Henry smiles.

> HENRY
> You don't like the title Life in the Woods?

> WALDO
> Simple titles, Henry. One word if possible. Nature. Experience. Self-Reliance.

> HENRY
> That's two words.

> WALDO
> It's hyphenated. Counts as one.

HENRY
I bow to your superior knowledge. As to hyphens.

Waldo sits and glances around the cabin.

HENRY
Anyway, why are you working on something new? I thought you were still reworking the other one. The river book.

HENRY
A Week on the Concord and Merrimack Rivers.

WALDO
Short titles, Henry. Short titles.

WALDO
I'll try to remember, Mr. Emerson.

WALDO
And three names. If you have them. Ralph Waldo Emerson. David Henry Thoreau. It adds gravity. We all need a little gravity.

HENRY
Henry David. You forget I changed it.

WALDO
Ah yes. Henry David Thoreau. Yes that sounds better. Perhaps I should have done that. Waldo Ralph Emerson?

Pause

BOTH
No.

WALDO
When you have Ralph and Waldo to choose from, I suppose it makes no difference.

HENRY
Emerson has a solid ring to it.

WALDO
Do you think?

HENRY
Oh yes.

WALDO
Perhaps. Perhaps you are just used to it.

HENRY
No one can pronounce Thoreau. They always put the accent on the second syllable.

WALDO
It is better to be famously mispronounced than to be pronounced infamous.

Henry pauses. Repeats the phrase to himself.

HENRY
That makes no sense.

Waldo pauses. Repeats the phrase to himself.

WALDO
True. It sounds good though.

HENRY
Fame is not something I shall ever know.

WALDO
It was not something I expected when I was a young minister in Boston. But here we are. Though some would say I am more infamous than famous.

HENRY
Ha.

WALDO
First the publication of my little Nature book, which caused so much ruckus. Then my Divinity School disaster.

HENRY
It was a fine speech.

WALDO
Lecture. Politicians give speeches.

HENRY
Sorry.

WALDO
They still won't allow me to speak at Harvard.

HENRY
Lecture. See I do listen.

Waldo laughs.

WALDO
Still.

HENRY
They don't know you.

WALDO
That is what fame is. Being widely unknown.

HENRY
That makes sense. I just can't quite figure out why.

WALDO
Fame.

Henry thinks.

HENRY
Rather than love, than money, than fame, give me truth.[17]

WALDO
All the toys that infatuate men, and which they play for,— houses, land, money, luxury, power, fame, are the selfsame thing, with a new gauze or two of illusion overlaid. [18]

They pause, thinking.

HENRY
You.

WALDO
I don't know. Yours has a power mine lacks, a straightforwardness. It reminds me of the way I used to write.

HENRY
A young man's phrase, you're saying. You think I will grow out of it?

WALDO
I hope not. I would write that way still if I could. If I still had that confidence. That clarity.

Waldo picks up a paper on the desk.

WALDO
Your essay on Thomas Carlyle? It was published?

---

[17] Thoreau, *Walden*
[18] Emerson, *Fate*

HENRY

It was. Though Mr. Greely is having trouble getting me paid for it.

WALDO

Lectures, Henry. That is what the public wants. And you get paid in advance.

HENRY

You do.

WALDO

Your lecture on Mr. Carlyle was well received. Many of our friends remarked on it.

HENRY

I don't think lecturing is for me.

WALDO

Why not?

HENRY

I can't say what I think.

WALDO

Since when? I have never known you to hold back your opinions. On anything.

Henry nods, and smiles.

HENRY

We have that in 'common'.

WALDO

I suppose we do.

HENRY

People don't like me.

WALDO
Everyone likes you, Henry. It's just.

HENRY
Yes?

WALDO
They don't understand you. You read all these languages, you are a fine poet, and could be the best surveyor in Massachusetts, yet you made pencils for a living.

HENRY
Those pencils were an excellent design. I made many improvements. I will stack my pencils up against any.

WALDO
You shouldn't be stacking pencils; you should be using them. This is what I'm saying Henry. Anything you do you do well. And yet what you do is. Well. People don't understand it.

HENRY
I don't need them to.

WALDO
And now this. Moving here. Building your cabin. It makes no sense to anyone.

HENRY
Channing approves.

WALDO
Don't tell me you are taking advice from William Ellery Channing.

HENRY
He has three names.

WALDO
Channing is simply happy he isn't the oddest person in Concord anymore.

HENRY
Is that what I am?

WALDO
Yes, Henry. Yes, you are without doubt the oddest person in a community of very odd people. Channing. Bronson Alcott. His daughter Louisa.

HENRY
Your Aunt Mary.

WALDO
I beg your pardon! Alright, yes. Though I would prefer for her the term exceptional.

HENRY
I would agree.

WALDO
Hawthorne is very odd.

HENRY
Odd? Is that the right word for him?

WALDO
Peculiar?

HENRY
Uncanny?

WALDO
Bizarre?

HENRY
Curious?

WALDO
Weird?

They pause.

TOGETHER
Weird.

HENRY
He is from Salem. They are all weird there.

WALDO
His wife Sophia[19] is from Salem also.

HENRY
Well. Perhaps not all.

WALDO
Another exceptional.

HENRY
Jones Very.

WALDO
He is not from here.

HENRY
He is of here.

WALDO
True. Poor Jones Very.

---

[19] Pronounced with a long I sound. So-Fy-Uh.

HENRY

Too much prophesy in his poetry.

WALDO

And yet the sanest mad man I ever met.

HENRY

Harvard will do that to you. Speaking of, Willie Goodwin.

WALDO

You think? I have some hopes for him.

HENRY

And then of course there is you.

WALDO

Me? I am not odd.

HENRY

Ha!

WALDO

I am not. I am normal. I am average. I simply think and read and write more than other people.

HENRY

You think that is not odd?

WALDO

I am the opposite of odd. With me it is simply too much normal. Which is why I attract so many odd people. They find me, like opposite poles.

HENRY

Like gravity. We all circle around you, but never approach, lest we burn up in the fire of your mind.

WALDO
Hardly. It sounds good though.

HENRY
Is that why I came to you?

WALDO
I couldn't say. Could you?

Nelly bustles in, full of purpose. Henry pauses, watching.

NELLY
Papa, the Captain has asked if you would read again after supper this evening.

WALDO
The captain?

He makes the mental transition. Slowly. Nelly waits patiently.

WALDO
Again? Surely they do not wish to be bored again.

NELLY
Everyone enjoyed it. And so did you.

WALDO
I suppose. It is more difficult now.

NELLY
I'll be there, Papa. Right next to you.

WALDO
Daughter. You should be living your own life, not sailing away with your fumbling father.

NELLY

Papa, this trip has been such a joy for me. How else could I have met the people we have met? Seen the places we have seen? London, Paris, Rome, Florence, and now Egypt. And to have you all to myself these months.

WALDO

We seem hardly ever to be by ourselves.

NELLY

Everyone wishes to see and be seen with the great Mr. Emerson. And to hear him. What will you read tonight?

WALDO

Must I?

NELLY

No. Of course not. I can explain to the captain.

WALDO

No. No. I will. I have earned my keep that way for fifty years. Why stop now? Perhaps he will refund our eight dollars.

NELLY

The passengers will be delighted.

WALDO

A bit of poetry perhaps?

NELLY

One of the short ones.

WALDO

Everything I write is short. I have a limited attention span.

NELLY

Oh yes.

WALDO
My longest work is only 90-some pages.

NELLY
Nature.

WALDO
Yes. I never had that stamina again. After that I realized it was easier to write short pieces and collect them. The Essays. English Traits. Representative Men. No one seems to have caught on yet.

NELLY
Well, you are a genius.

WALDO
And quotes. Always quote other writers. It lengthens the piece and it makes people think you know more than you do.

NELLY
So short works, lots of quotes. That's how you became the most famous American thinker since Benjamin Franklin.

WALDO
That. And your mother. If I had not found her, at the time. I don't know. I think my life would have been very different.

NELLY
At the very least, you would be on his journey with some other daughter.

Waldo laughs, sorts through the manuscripts on the desk[20], picks one up, turns the pages, reads.

---

[20] Emerson always read his lectures.

                                WALDO
Give All to Love by Ralph Waldo Emerson. Three names.
Very good.

   Nelly looks at him, puzzled again.

                                WALDO
Give all to love;
Obey thy heart;
Friends, kindred, days,
Estate, good-fame,
Plans, credit and the Muse,—
Nothing refuse.

'T is a brave master;
Let it have scope:
Follow it utterly,
Hope beyond hope:
High and more high
It dives into noon,
With wing unspent,
Untold intent:
But it is a god,
Knows its own path
And the outlets of the sky.

It was never for the mean;
It requireth courage stout.
Souls above doubt,
Valor unbending,
It will reward,—
They shall return
More than they were,
And ever ascending.

Leave all for love;
Yet, hear me, yet,
One word more thy heart behoved,
One pulse more of firm endeavor,—
Keep thee to-day,
To-morrow, forever,
Free as an Arab
Of thy beloved.

Cling with life to the maid;
But when the surprise,
First vague shadow of surmise
Flits across her bosom young,
Of a joy apart from thee,
Free be she, fancy-free;
Nor thou detain her vesture's hem,
Nor the palest rose she flung
From her summer diadem.

Though thou loved her as thyself,
As a self of purer clay,
Though her parting dims the day,
Stealing grace from all alive;
Heartily know,
When half-gods go,
The gods arrive.

NELLY

That's lovely, but perhaps too short?

WALDO

No such thing.

NELLY
I think they might prefer one of your essays.

WALDO
One of the older ones perhaps. Self-Reliance.

He picks up another manuscript, turns the pages. Nelly tries to interject but he goes ahead.

WALDO
I read the other day some verses written by an eminent painter which were original and not conventional. The soul always hears an admonition in such lines, let the subject be what it may. The sentiment they instill is of more value than any thought they may contain. To believe our own thought, to believe that what is true for you in your private heart is true for all men, -- that is genius.

He pauses.

WALDO
I like that one. It reminds me of who I used to think I could be.

NELLY
Papa, you read that one last night.

WALDO
I thought it sounded familiar. Too often these days my own words return as strangers.

He turns more pages.

WALDO
My essay on Experience?

NELLY
Oh Papa. Not that one.

WALDO
I am surprised that you remember it. You are very young when it was published.

NELLY
I remember it. But.
> *She looks through the other books on the desk.*

How about something from Representative Men? The piece on Goethe perhaps?

Waldo reads.

WALDO
Experience. By Ralph Waldo Emerson.

Waldo acts as if he is at podium giving a lecture.

WALDO
Where do we find ourselves? In a series of which we do not know the extremes, and believe that it has none. We wake and find ourselves on a stair; there are stairs below us, which we seem to have ascended; there are stairs above us, many a one, which go upward and out of sight. But the Genius which, according to the old belief, stands at the door by which we enter, and gives us the lethe to drink, that we may tell no tales, mixed the cup too strongly, and we cannot shake off the lethargy now at noonday. Sleep lingers all our lifetime about our eyes, as night hovers all day in the boughs of the fir-tree. All things swim and glitter. Our life is not so much threatened as our perception. Ghostlike we glide through nature, and should not know our place again. Did our birth fall in some fit of indigence and frugality in nature, that she

was so sparing of her fire and so liberal of her earth, that it appears to us that we lack the affirmative principle, and though we have health and reason, yet we have no superfluity of spirit for new creation? We have enough to live and bring the year about, but not an ounce to impart or to invest. Ah that our Genius were a little more of a genius! We are like millers on the lower levels of a stream, when the factories above them have exhausted the water. We too fancy that the upper people must have raised their dams.

Waldo starts to weaken, to fumble, to forget.

WALDO

If any of us knew what we were doing, or where we are going, then when we think we best know! We do not know today whether we are busy or idle. In times when we thought ourselves indolent, we have afterwards discovered, that much was accomplished, and much was begun in us. All our days are so unprofitable while they pass, that 'tis wonderful where or when we ever got anything of this which we call wisdom, poetry, virtue.

Nelly steadies his hands.

WALDO

Some heavenly days must have been intercalated somewhere, like those that Hermes won with dice of the Moon, that Osiris might be born. It is said, all martyrdoms looked mean when they were suffered. Every ship is a romantic object, except that we sail in. Embark, and the romance quits our vessel, and hangs on every other sail in the horizon. Our life looks trivial, and we shun to record it. Men seem to have learned of the horizon the art of perpetual retreating and reference.

Waldo loses his place.

NELLY

How many individuals can we count in society? how many actions? how many opinions? So much of our time is preparation, so much is routine, and so much retrospect, that the pith of each man's genius contracts itself to a very few hours.

Waldo gains strength again.

WALDO

The history of literature—take the net result of Tiraboschi, Warton, or Schlegel,—is a sum of very few ideas, and of very few original tales, —all the rest being variation of these. So in this great society wide lying around us, a critical analysis would find very few spontaneous actions. It is almost all custom and gross sense. There are even few opinions, and these seem organic in the speakers, and do not disturb the—

Waldo falters.

HENRY
Whispering

Universal necessity.

WALDO

Universal necessity. What opium is instilled into all disaster! It shows formidable as we approach it, but there is at last no rough rasping friction, but the most slippery sliding surfaces. We fall soft on a thought. Ate Dea[21] is gentle.

Waldo stops. Nelly takes the book and reads. Lights up on Ellen.

---

[21] Ate is the Greek Goddess of Delusion.

NELLY

The only thing grief has taught me, is to know how shallow it is. That, like all the rest, plays about the surface, and never introduces me into the reality, for contact with which, we would even pay the costly price of sons and lovers. Was it Boscovich who found out that bodies never come in contact? Well, souls never touch their objects. An innavigable sea washes with silent waves between us and the things we aim at and converse with.

She offers him the book, points to the passage.

ELLEN

Grief too will make us idealists.

Waldo gathers, goes on.

WALDO

In the death of my son, now more than two years ago, I seem to have lost a beautiful estate, — no more. I cannot get it nearer to me. If tomorrow I should be informed of the bankruptcy of my principal debtors, the loss of my property would be a great inconvenience to me, perhaps, for many years; but it would leave me as it found me, — neither better nor worse. So is it with this calamity: it does not touch me: some thing which I fancied was a part of me, which could not be torn away without tearing me, nor enlarged without enriching me, falls off from me, and leaves no scar. It was caducous. I grieve that grief can teach me nothing, nor carry me one step into real nature.

He stops again.

HENRY
The Indian who was laid under a curse, that the wind should not blow on him, nor water flow to him, nor fire burn him, is a type of us all. The dearest events are summer-rain, and we the Para coats that shed every drop. Nothing is left us now but death. We look to that with a grim satisfaction, saying, there at least is reality that will not dodge us.

ELLEN
Dream delivers us to dream, and there is no end to illusion.

Waldo closes the manuscript.

WALDO
Yes. Yes. One of the more recent ones then. My essay on Memory perhaps?

He smiles. Nelly nods and comforts him, then exits.

HENRY
You never told me what you thought of it.

WALDO
Thought of what?

HENRY
My essay on Carlyle.

WALDO
Ah. Well done. I said so.

HENRY
Exactly. You shook my hand. You said I did well. But you never said what you thought.

WALDO
That is unusual for me.

HENRY
One might even say odd.

Waldo smiles.

WALDO
One might. Well, it is difficult for me to judge. You know only the words. I know the man.

HENRY
Does that make a difference? It was his words I was writing about.

WALDO
It is hard for me to be objective.

HENRY
Why?

WALDO
The man is a friend.

HENRY
You can't be objective because he is a friend?

WALDO
I don't know.

HENRY
Are you objective with me?

WALDO
It is not the same.

HENRY
You have no trouble criticizing me. You and Margaret Fuller made something of a sport of it.

WALDO
The pieces you sent to the Dial, they, we, wanted to help. We see so much promise in you Henry.

HENRY
You keep saying that. Of course I know that, Mr. Emerson. I am grateful to you, and to Miss Fuller.

WALDO
We want to see the remarkable abilities we know you possess reach fullness. Maturity.

HENRY
As do I. Why do you think I came out here?

WALDO
I haven't the slightest idea.

HENRY
Don't you?

WALDO
Didn't you like staying with us, Henry?

HENRY
Of course I did. You know I did.

WALDO
I thought you did. Everything was in its right place. Everything worked.

HENRY
For you.

WALDO
But not for you?

HENRY
It was not my place. It was not my home. It was not my. Family.

WALDO
We all cared for you Henry. The children. Mrs. Emerson.

HENRY
I know. I.

Henry stops. He is getting into dangerous territory.

HENRY
So? What did you think of my lecture?

WALDO
I wish you had left me out of it.

HENRY
How? How can I leave you out of anything? You are Ralph Waldo Emerson.

WALDO
The man who is banished forever from Harvard Divinity School.

HENRY
The American Plato.

WALDO
The man who is foolish enough to spend his life writing and thinking. Usually in that order.

HENRY
The successor to Montaigne. The genius of Concord.

Henry pauses.

HENRY
Genius.

WALDO
In every work of genius we recognize our own rejected thoughts.[22]

HENRY
You're quoting yourself.

WALDO
It's hard not to.

HENRY
It breaks the rules.

WALDO
Were there rules?

Henry stares.

WALDO
Fine.

Waldo stares back, discerning.

WALDO
At first glance he measured his companion, and, though insensible to some fine traits of culture, could very well report his weight and caliber. And this made the impression of genius which his conversation sometimes gave.[23]

---

[22] Emerson, Self-Reliance
[23] Emerson, *Tribute* to Thoreau, Atlantic Magazine, 1862

HENRY

It takes a man of genius to travel in his own country, in his native village; to make any progress between his door and his gate.[24]

> *Waldo shakes his head, tired of the game.*

WALDO

I cannot judge.

HENRY

You cannot not. You are everywhere for me. Except here. In this cabin.

WALDO

Except that I am here.

HENRY

But at least I am also here. I am myself here. This is my place. This pond is my pond. These beans are my beans. And I am finding my way here. To something different.

WALDO

Different from me, you mean.

HENRY

There is only one Ralph Waldo Emerson.

> *Long pause.*

WALDO

How are the beans this year?

---

[24] Thoreau, Journal 1851

HENRY
The late freeze took the crop. Until then I expected twelve bushels.

WALDO
Fertilizer?

HENRY
None. Except the mold left over from the stumps when I pulled them.

WALDO
Economical.

HENRY
Of necessity.

Waldo looks slyly at Henry.

WALDO
Necessity.

Pause.

HENRY
The better part of the man is soon plowed into the soil for compost. By a seeming fate, commonly called necessity, they are employed, as it says in an old book, laying up treasures which moth and rust will corrupt and thieves break through and steal.[25]

---

[25] Thoreau, *Walden*

WALDO
We are sure, that, though we know not how, necessity does comport with liberty, the individual with the world, my polarity with the spirit of the times.[26]

They pause.

HENRY
You.

Waldo nods.

WALDO
Henry.

HENRY
Of necessity.

Waldo walks around the cabin, inspecting.

WALDO
The cabin is holding up well.

HENRY
You have not visited in a while, Mr. Emerson.

WALDO
I did not wish to disturb your work. You said you were making progress.

HENRY
I was. I am. I think.

Henry pauses.

---

[26] Emerson, *Fate*

WALDO
How much longer do you plan to stay?

HENRY
That is up to you.

WALDO
How do you mean?

HENRY
This is your land.

WALDO
Henry. Please. I don't wish to argue. At least not about that.

HENRY
We are who we are.

WALDO
As you say. I wanted you to know that I am going away.

HENRY
West? South?

WALDO
East. Back to Europe.

HENRY
How long?

WALDO
Six months this time. Possibly longer.

Pause

HENRY
When?

WALDO

September.

HENRY

Impossible. What of your trees sir?

WALDO

My orchard you mean?

HENRY

You may possibly get in your peaches by then, the Early Rose and the Presidents. And your pears may well be fine, the Seckels and the Bloodgoods certainly. But what of your apples? The Gravensteins, the Bellflowers. and the Hightops? And the quince. Don't get me started on the quince.

WALDO

I have been very concerned about the quince. You know I love my quince apple pie. Mrs. Emerson's pies are the wonder of New England.

HENRY

I remember.

WALDO

So I thought. I was hoping. We all, the family, you see, were hoping. The orchard has never fared so well as when you were tending it, Henry.

HENRY

No.

WALDO

Your apple needs you, Henry. The one you grew, the one we named for you. The Thoreau is wasting away in your absence.

HENRY

I have my work here.

WALDO
I don't understand this choice, Henry. When you asked to build out here, I agreed. But I didn't understand. I still don't.

HENRY
My work is here.

WALDO
You are a talented poet.

HENRY
I'm not a poet. I don't know what I am but it isn't a poet.

WALDO
Then write something else.

HENRY
I'm trying.

WALDO
Solitude is necessary. I understand that. But isolation? For one with your temperament. Is that wise?

Henry pauses.

HENRY
Wisdom.

WALDO
Henry.

HENRY
Wisdom.

WALDO
Can't we?

HENRY
Wisdom.

WALDO
To finish the moment, to find the journey's end in every step of the road, to live the greatest number of good hours, is wisdom.[27]

HENRY
How insufficient is all wisdom without love[28].

Neither speaks for a moment.

WALDO
The children miss you Henry.

HENRY
I still see them.

WALDO
Mrs. Emerson misses you.

HENRY
I miss them all.

WALDO
Then come home, Henry.

HENRY
It isn't my home. I will never have a home. Not in that sense. Nor wife. Nor children. I know that now. It is not a life meant for me. Or a life I wasn't meant for.

---

[27] Emerson, *Experience*
[28] Thoreau, *Journals*

                          WALDO
You don't have to make that choice. I know there is a pressure. Yes there are compromises. Distractions. Interruptions. From the work we do. But they are necessary. I don't know how to say it. I'm not speaking of love.

                          HENRY
Don't, sir.

                          WALDO
A life together. Children. The things they teach you. The foundation they give you.

                          HENRY
I saw that foundation crumble.

  Waldo pauses, sinks into a chair.

                          HENRY
I loved him too.

                          WALDO
He was a wondrous child.

                          HENRY
I saw him suffer just as you did.

                          WALDO
My deep-eyed boy.

                          HENRY
I saw him die.

                          WALDO
My Waldo.

                          HENRY
The same year.

WALDO

I know.

HENRY

The same year.

WALDO

I'm sorry.

HENRY

The same year as John.

WALDO

Your brother was. We all.

HENRY

Waldo from scarlet fever and John from tetanus.

WALDO

I have never left that room.

HENRY

Five years ago.

WALDO

Is it five?

HENRY

The year your essays were published. I don't know how you managed it. I don't know. How you could.

WALDO

It's what we do.

HENRY

It is. Yes.

WALDO

It's what we must do.

HENRY

It's what I am doing.

WALDO

Necessity.

HENRY

Necessity.

WALDO

If so say so Henry. I don't understand, but I do trust.

HENRY

You see what you invite me back to.

WALDO

My boy. Can't you see that…

HENRY

No. It is not that way, with us. That's not who we are.

WALDO

As you say.

HENRY

I have loved.

WALDO

It's not important.

HENRY

I have loved.

WALDO

Yes yes.

HENRY

I still love.

WALDO

Mrs. Emerson.

Henry turns quickly.

HENRY

Sir?

WALDO

Mrs. Emerson. She would.

HENRY

Yes.

WALDO

She wished me to ask.

HENRY

Yes.

WALDO

Mrs. Emerson would like some beans. If there are any left. That is what I came to ask.

HENRY

Really?

WALDO

She would take me to task if I forgot.

HENRY

For.

WALDO

You know Lidian.

HENRY

I know Mrs. Emerson.

Waldo walks slowly to the door. Stops.

Henry pauses. Deciding.

HENRY
What I have, I'll bring.

WALDO
I know you will. I don't understand, Henry. But I do trust.

Waldo hands the papers back to Henry, then starts to leave. He stops at the door.

WALDO
Henry.

HENRY
Yes, Mr. Emerson?

WALDO
I am not objective.

HENRY
Sir?

WALDO
About you. I am not objective about you.

Henry waits.

WALDO
I believe that I am less objective about you than any friend I have ever had.

HENRY
I'll keep that in mind, Mr. Emerson.

WALDO
Do please, Mr. Thoreau.

Lights fades on Henry.

WALDO
Good spot for a cabin. I hope it lasts.

ELLEN
It does.

Lights up on Ellen.

ELLEN
It will.

WALDO
How do you know?

ELLEN
It will be a monument.

WALDO
A marker.

ELLEN
A memory.

WALDO
Something to be lost.

ELLEN
Something to become.

WALDO
And is there value in that?

Ellen

In the solitude to which every man is always returning, he has a sanity and revelations, which in his passage into new worlds he will carry with him.

> *Lights up on Louisa, sitting at Emerson's desk, trying to light the lamp.*

Louisa

Let there be light.

> *Waldo walks into the scene. Louisa stands quickly and moves to him.*

Louisa

Excuse me, Mr. Emerson. My **father sent me to ask about little Waldo**.

> *Waldo extinguishes the match.*

Waldo

He is dead, child.

> *Louisa doesn't respond. Waldo goes to the desk and begins writing.*

Waldo

Tell Mr. Alcott I will write to him.

> *Louisa stands a moment, trembling. Waldo doesn't notice. Louisa turns to leave, then collapses.*

Waldo.

Louisa!

> *Waldo rushes to her.*

WALDO.
I am sorry, child. I am. Not myself.

He helps her to a chair.

WALDO.
Henry!

Henry enters.

WALDO.
Henry, would you bring Louisa some water. She is feeling unsteady.

He looks at Louisa, nods, and quickly leaves.

WALDO.
He doesn't say much, our Henry. At the best of times. Which this is not.

LOUISA
You shall miss him.

WALDO.
The old should not survive the young.

LOUISA
Are you very old? My father is.

WALDO.
Your father is wise. That makes him seem old.

LOUISA
Are you wise?

WALDO.
Not today.

Henry enters with water, hands the cup to Louisa,

smiling sadly, then leaves.

LOUISA
He is sad.

WALDO
He loved my son. He was so good about spending time with him. They would wander through the orchard for hours sometimes, and Henry would explain all about the trees and the fruit, which were sweet, which were tart, which made the best pies. Waldo was curious about everything. And he loved pies, like his father.

LOUISA
His brother died. Lockjaw, my father said.

WALDO
Henry's brother John. Yes. Tragic. Just recently he made a remarkable daguerreotype of Waldo. To lose them both.

Waldo pauses, lost in thought.

LOUISA
Are you sad?

Waldo pauses again, thinking.

WALDO
I am sure I will be.

Louisa thinks about that.

LOUISA
I am sad.

Lidian enters, watching from the doorway.

LOUISA
I am so sorry about Waldo. He was lovely and good. He always minded when I watched him. I shall miss him.

WALDO.
Will you?

She nods.

LOUISA
He is with God now.

At this Waldo starts to break. He gathers himself and starts to speak. Lidian strides in, furious.

LIDIAN.
Don't you dare. Don't you dare, Mr. Emerson. Don't you tell her my son is not in Heaven. Don't you dare tell her that.

She can't continue.

Waldo gets up and walks to her. They look at each other, do not touch.

WALDO.
Henry!

Henry enters. Waldo's eyes do not leave Lidian.

WALDO.
Henry, will you see Louisa home?

HENRY.
Of course, Mr. Emerson.

Waldo takes Lidian's arm. She pulls away. He rests a hand gently on her shoulder and guides her out of the room. Before leaving, he stops and turns to Louisa.

WALDO.
Wherever he is, I believe that God is with him.

LOUISA
Well. That's alright then.

Waldo and Lidian leave. Thoreau sits on the floor near Louisa. They are silent for a moment.

LOUISA
He has wonderful books, doesn't he?

HENRY
Yes. Many.

Louisa stands. Thoreau looks at her sharply. But she seems fine. He relaxes.

LOUISA
He lets me borrow them sometimes.

She walks to the desk, picks up a book.

LOUISA
And sometimes I read the ones he sends to my father.

HENRY
That's good, Louisa.

LOUISA
My father believes that even girls deserve a fine education.

HENRY
I agree with him. Your father is a wise man.

LOUISA
So everyone says. He teaches us himself. In our home.

She picks up another book, glances through it.

LOUISA
I have even read Mr. Emerson book.

Henry looks up at this, amused.

HENRY
What did you think?

She puts the book back.

LOUISA
He quotes from other writers too often. A good writer shouldn't need to quote others. He should say what he has to say himself.

HENRY
I'll keep that in mind.

She picks up another book, weighs it in her hand, puts it back.

LOUISA
Too heavy. Books shouldn't be too heavy. They should be light enough to carry in one's pocket.

HENRY
I'll keep that in mind too. Any more advice for writers?

LOUISA
Don't be boring.

Henry rises.

LOUISA
I shall write about pirates I think.

HENRY
Do you know any pirates?

LOUISA
Not yet. But I am only nine. So far.

HENRY
You have time.

LOUISA
I hope so. Waldo didn't.

HENRY
No. I suppose not.

LOUISA
I had a brother.

HENRY
You did?

LOUISA
He died. But still.

HENRY
Yes. Still. Brothers are important.

LOUISA
I have three sisters.

HENRY
You could write about them.

LOUISA
Too boring.

HENRY
I think maybe boring books are the ones people most need to read.

LOUISA
Like what?

HENRY
I don't know. What is the most boring thing you can think of.

She thinks,

LOUISA
Beans.

HENRY
Beans?

LOUISA
Father says it is wrong to eat meat. So we eat a lot of beans. They are very boring.

HENRY
Beans. Hmmm.

LOUISA
I bet pirates don't eat beans.

HENRY
You might be surprised. Beans keep very well on a sea voyage.

LOUISA
My pirates won't eat beans.

Waldo enters.

HENRY
All writing is making choices.

Henry nods to Waldo.

HENRY
Or so I have heard.

                    WALDO

All life is making choices. Unless they are made for you.

    Henry stands.

                    WALDO

Henry. Mrs. Emerson is asking for you.

                    HENRY

For me?

                    WALDO

Perhaps you will have more luck in comforting her. I don't seem to have that skill.

                    HENRY

Of course.

    He leaves.

                    WALDO

Louisa, Henry will walk you home a bit later. Is that all right? I shall write a note to your father explaining.

                    WALDO

Yes Mr. Emerson.

    Waldo goes to his table and starts writing. Louisa moves
    quietly to the table and watches him.

                    LOUISA

Mr. Emerson?

    Not looking up.

                    WALDO

Yes Louisa?

LOUISA
Shall I go in and see to Ellen?

WALDO
No dear.

LOUISA
I have cared for her before.

WALDO
Yes I remember. You are an excellent nurse. Perhaps that shall be your career.

LOUISA
Perhaps. Can you make money at it?

WALDO
I suppose a bit. Do you need money?

LOUISA
Our family always seems to.

WALDO
That is certainly true.

LOUISA
Why is that?

WALDO
Pardon?

LOUISA
If my father is so wise, why do we never have any money? Can't wise people make money?

WALDO
Not usually. No. Most people who are wise are also poor.

                    LOUISA
Why is that?

                    WALDO
Because I suppose they have better things to do than make money.

                    LOUISA
Are you wise?

                    WALDO
Not today.

                    LOUISA
Are you poor?

                    WALDO
Not if I finish this essay. And the next one. And the next one.

   Louisa walks up to the desk and looks at the lecture.

                    LOUISA
You can make money from writing?

                    WALDO
Only if you finish it.

                    LOUISA
I shall be a writer then.

                    WALDO
Good for you dear.

                    LOUISA
I shall write about pirates. Who don't eat beans.

   Waldo looks up.

WALDO
I don't believe I have ever read anything like that.

LOUISA
I shall be an original.

WALDO
Like your father.

LOUISA
I shall be an original who makes money.

WALDO
An excellent plan.

LOUISA
It is.

WALDO
You are surrounded by originals. The most original moralist at present in America is your father.

LOUISA
Someone should give him a pension.

WALDO
You have met my friend Ms. Fuller I believe. She is another original.

LOUISA
She talks too.

WALDO
Pardon?

LOUISA
Like my father. She hosts Conversations. Can you make money talking?

WALDO

Sometimes. Politicians seem to do quite well. But I don't think you can be one.

LOUISA

Why not?

WALDO

You can't vote.

LOUISA

Why not?

WALDO

You can't own property.

LOUISA

Who says so?

WALDO

The laws of Massachusetts say so.

LOUISA

Who makes the laws?

WALDO

Politicians.

LOUISA

Who are men.

WALDO

Exactly.

LOUISA

It all seems very suspicious to me.

WALDO
I suppose it is. But perhaps you will feel different when you are married.

LOUISA
Oh I shall never marry.

WALDO
Why is that?

LOUISA
My father needs me.

Waldo goes back to his writing.

WALDO
You may feel differently when you are older.

LOUISA
I might. I doubt he will.

He looks up and smiles.

WALDO
You may be right. Daughters are a comfort to their fathers.

Waldo goes back to his work.

WALDO
You remind me of someone.

LOUISA
Who?

WALDO
I can't remember. Louisa, perhaps you could ask cook to make a cup of tea, and then you could bring it to Mrs. Emerson. She might find it a comfort.

                LOUISA
Yes Mr. Emerson.

   Louisa starts to go, then stops.

                LOUISA
Why don't you?

                WALDO
Pardon?

                LOUISA
You wished to comfort Mrs. Emerson, and you think a cup of tea would be comforting. Why don't you bring it to her?

                WALDO
That is something else you will understand when you are married.

                LOUISA
I have said I shall not marry, so perhaps you should explain it to me now.

Waldo pauses, thinking, then says:

                WALDO
Henry.

                LOUISA
Where?

                WALDO
That is who you remind me of. Henry.

                LOUISA
Really? I don't think we look much alike. He is older and almost has a beard.

   Emerson tries not to smile.

WALDO
So he does. I merely mean that he has an endless supply of questions.

LOUISA
They are only endless because no one gives me the answers.

WALDO
No one ever gives answers, Louisa. They always come at a cost.

Louisa digs in her pocket and puts some coins on the desk.

LOUISA
Three cents worth please.

Waldo smiles, then sighs. He starts to break, then collects himself.

WALDO
I don't know that I have so many today.

LOUISA
Mr. Emerson, you are said to be a very fine explainer. Will you not explain to me why a cup of tea from me is comforting and a cup from you is not? I believe this could be very important to my future happiness.

Waldo picks up the coins.

WALDO
For three pennies, I shall give you three answers. Is that fair?
He holds up one penny.
First, because you are not her husband and she is not your wife.
He puts down the first penny and picks up the second.
Second, because I am her husband, and she is my wife.
He puts down the second penny and picks up the third.
Third, because I am her first husband, and she is my second wife.
Louisa thinks.

LOUISA
I should like my three cents back please.

WALDO
I don't blame you.

He gives them back.

LOUISA
Families are very complicated in my opinion.

Waldo begins writing again.

WALDO
Perhaps that is what you should write about.

Louisa thinks.

LOUISA
I suppose pirates have families.

WALDO
I'm sure they do.

LOUISA
I still don't understand why you aren't sad. Mrs. Emerson is sad. I am sad. Mr. Thoreau is sad. Why aren't you?

Waldo thinks for a moment.

WALDO
Because I am broken.

LOUISA
What does that mean? You are Mr. Emerson. How can you be broken?

WALDO
My father died when I was your age. My wife, Ellen, the first Ellen, died when we had been just few months married. My brother Edward died shortly after. Then Charles. Charles. You are too young to remember him. Charles was the real genius of the Emerson family. I have never met anyone like him. But.

He pauses.

LOUISA
I'm sorry.

WALDO
When that is your life. Loss after loss after loss. And when you are a particular kind of person, a particular kind of man. Something in you breaks. Your heart disconnects. And you left alone in your mind. Forever.

LOUISA
That sounds awful.

WALDO

It is. But because of it I can do things that most other people can't.

LOUISA

So it is a cost.

WALDO

Yes. A cost. I try and make the best of it.

LOUISA

And Mrs. Emerson is not broken. So she can be sad.

WALDO

Mrs. Emerson is. The best woman. The best wife.

LOUISA

I don't think I will get married. Not even to a pirate. Father and mother adore each other and are miserable. You and Mrs. Emerson.

WALDO

You are a very perceptive child, Louisa. That may not lead you to a happy life.

LOUISA

Are there any?

Henry enters.

HENRY

Mr. Emerson, Ellen has a fever also.

WALDO

What? No.

He gets up to go.

WALDO
Henry, you will please see Louisa home?

HENRY
Of course.

WALDO
Then come right back. She will need you.

Waldo starts to leave.

LOUISA
Mr. Emerson?

He stops.

LOUISA
You comfort me.

Waldo smiles.

WALDO
Thank you, Louisa.

He turns to go, turns back.

WALDO
You should write about families. Just not mine.

Lights fade on Louisa and Henry.

ELLEN
You have comforted many.

Waldo smiles at the sound.

Lights up on Ellen.

WALDO
Do you think so?

ELLEN
His sterling values will presently recall the eye and thought of the best minds, and his books will be reprinted and read anew by coming generations.

WALDO
Ah. Books.

ELLEN
You comforted me.

WALDO
Did I?

ELLEN
Shall I remind you?

He turns to her.

WALDO
Yes. Remind me. Please. Remind me.

ELLEN
We met on Christmas day. You were my favorite gift.

She moves to the sofa and sits.

ELLEN
I was a woman of 16 and you were a boy of 24.

She motions to him and he joins her.

ELLEN

We spoke of Byron. You thought I meant the poet and I thought you meant my spaniel. We were very confused for a moment, and then your stern and serious ministerial face crinkled up and you laughed and laughed. And I decided then and there that you would marry me.

WALDO

You had a dog named Byron.

ELLEN

That you remember! I would be insulted but he was a very good dog.

WALDO

Byron. Funny.

ELLEN

A year later you brought me a book called *Forget Me Not*. A year! Now that is funny.

WALDO

That is ironic. It's not the same.

ELLEN

What is ironic is that I grew up in Concord, New Hampshire, and after I died you settled in Concord, Massachusetts.

WALDO

That is not ironic. It is a coincidence, and possibly a metaphor.

ELLEN

I wanted to be a poet and you wanted to be a minister. You ended up a poet and I ended up a memory. What is that?

WALDO

That is a tragedy.

ELLEN
Oh, your poetry is not that bad.

He looks at her.

WALDO
That is funny.

She curtsies.

ELLEN
Are they coming back?

WALDO
What?

ELLEN
The memories.

WALDO
Oh they come back occasionally. They don't stay.

ELLEN
Shall I?

WALDO
What?

ELLEN
Stay?

He looks offstage where Nelly has exited.

WALDO
Ellen is...

ELLEN
I am Ellen.

WALDO
You are Ellinelli. You are Lady Frolick and Lady Pensero.

ELLEN
I believe so.

WALDO
I remember something that I have forgotten.

ELLEN
You had forgotten but now you remember?

WALDO
No, I remember that I have forgotten.

ELLEN
I see.

WALDO
I have tried and tried.

ELLEN
Yes?

WALDO
For some time, I have tried.

ELLEN
Yes?

WALDO
I cannot recall.

ELLEN
Say it.

WALDO
Your face. I cannot recall your face.

ELLEN
Is that all?

WALDO
I want to. Very much. But I cannot.

ELLEN
I'm almost glad. I was not so beautiful toward the end. So pale and thin.

WALDO
You were always beautiful.

ELLEN
But wait. You have my miniature still?

WALDO
Your picture. Yes. I have it in my study. Or I did. Who knows where it is now? I don't think it burned. Though that night was so confusing.

ELLEN
If you have the miniature, then you can't have forgotten how I looked.

WALDO
I look at the painting. Often. But I do not recognize you when I see it.

ELLEN
Was it not a good likeness?

WALDO
It's not that. It just doesn't feel the same.

ELLEN
The same?

WALDO
As when I looked at you. I still remember the way I felt. Transcendent.

ELLEN
Transcendent? You make me sound very grand.

WALDO
You were.

ELLEN
Transcendent? No. I was a girl in love, for the first and only time. You mistake transcendent for incandescent.

Her lighting brightens a bit.

WALDO
Transcendent sounds better.

ELLEN
You're just used to it[29].

WALDO
Perhaps.

ELLEN
I suppose I was a little transcendent, towards the end. It was so hard to hold on to life. I tried, for you.

WALDO
You were brave. I remember that.

ELLEN
We had so little time. I didn't want to waste it in tears.

---

[29] Emerson was the founder of American Transcendentalism.

WALDO
And your cough. Your terrible cough. And the blood. So much blood from such a tiny body.

ELLEN
I am healed now.

WALDO
I took you south, to try the climate.

ELLEN
To Philadelphia!

WALDO
And I had to leave you there and return to Boston. I have never felt so alone.

ELLEN
I was the one in Philadelphia.

WALDO
And I was desperate to know if you missed me as much as I missed you.

ELLEN
That is natural. You were so young.

WALDO
Natural. You were young. Was I ever young?

ELLEN
You were. You just didn't know it.

WALDO
I feel younger now, with you here.

ELLEN
Memories are not miniatures.

WALDO
What are they? I don't remember.

ELLEN
Memory is a presumption of a possession of the future. Now we are halves, we see the past but not the future, but in that day will the hemisphere complete itself and foresight be as perfect as aftersight.[30]

WALDO
Did I write that?

ELLEN
Of course.

WALDO
It is like your face. Though I know it, I don't recognize it.

ELLEN
I like that one especially. It reminds me of your sermons. One of the saddest parts of being sick was that I could not attend your sermons.

WALDO
It reminds you?

ELLEN
You were so grand in the pulpit with your high cloak and sweet voice. And only once per sermon would you let yourself sneak a glance at your Ellinelli. And when you did look on my face, only for a second and with no smile or nod or sign, I knew I needed no other communion.

WALDO
Nor I.

---

[30] *Essay on Memory*, Emerson

He turns suddenly.

WALDO
I remember!

Ellen turns away.

ELLEN
My face?

WALDO
For a year afterwards, I walked each day to your grave.

He turns to her.

ELLEN
Poor Waldo.

WALDO
You asked me to.

ELLEN
Did I?

WALDO
Breathe not yet, but wait until
My spirit is set free.
Then whisper round my grave
The tale of my release —[31]

ELLEN
I wrote that.

WALDO
You did.

---

[31] *To the South Wind*, Ellen Emerson

ELLEN
And you remember.

WALDO
I do.

ELLEN
But you cannot recall my face.

WALDO
No. I remember I walked each day to your grave.

He takes a step toward her.

WALDO
I needed to see your face. Once more.

Another step. Dimmer.

WALDO
Just once more.

Another step, and he is near her.

WALDO
One day I entered your tomb.

She turns to him.

WALDO
And opened the coffin.

He reaches up to her veil.

WALDO
And I saw.

Her light goes out. He lowers his arm.

WALDO
Nothing.

ELLEN
Nothing?

WALDO
Nothing.

ELLEN
It was empty?

WALDO
We were in darkness.

ELLEN
That is natural.

WALDO
Natural. Yes. Does it bother you?

ELLEN
What?

WALDO
That I, came to see you?

ELLEN
I come often to see you.

WALDO
Are you sure you are not a ghost?

ELLEN
Maybe a memory is a ghost that lives inside us.

WALDO
Maybe a ghost is a memory that lives outside us.

ELLEN
But you don't believe in the immortality of the soul.

WALDO
Maybe that is where memories go. The afterlife belongs not to us but to them.

She steps into the light again. Her veil is lifted.

ELLEN
Perhaps they are us.

WALDO
After you died, I resigned from the ministry. I was lost, so I thought I may as well be lost somewhere new.

ELLEN
Clever Waldo.

WALDO
That's a new one. I wandered for a year. Syracuse. Naples. Rome. Florence. Paris. London.

ELLEN
So far from home.

WALDO
Without you I had no home.

ELLEN
So far then.

WALDO
I met great writers that I had admired: Landor, Coleridge, Wordsworth, Carlyle.

ELLEN
Your Heroes.

WALDO
I found them to be…just men.

ELLEN
You were disappointed.

WALDO
Yes. But. It is a kind of freedom, to learn what is possible, and by whom.

ELLEN
It is.

WALDO
By the end I knew something in me had changed, but I did not know what.

ELLEN
I know.

WALDO
I came back, to Concord. I could not return to Boston and the church.

ELLEN
I understand.

WALDO
I had to make a living, so I started writing, and speaking.

She smiles.

ELLEN
Lecturing.

And he smiles.

WALDO

Lecturing. I married Lidian.

ELLEN

A good woman.

WALDO

A good woman.

ELLEN

You needed her.

WALDO

I loved her. Love her. You can tell her I said so.

ELLEN

You can tell her.

WALDO

I can tell her.

ELLEN

She gave you children.

WALDO

Ellen. Edith. Edward. Poor Waldo, gone so young.

ELLEN

Poor Waldo. So much of tragedy.

WALDO

So much of life.

ELLEN

If I had not gotten sick...

WALDO

I could not have left you.

ELLEN
Maybe that is why I had to leave you.

WALDO
Let us build altars to the Beautiful Necessity.[32]

ELLEN
Though thou loved her as thyself,
As a self of purer clay,
Though her parting dims the day,
Stealing grace from all alive;[33]

WALDO
Heartily know,
When half-gods go,
The gods arrive. [17]

ELLEN
It is all right.

WALDO
I remember.

ELLEN
The loving. And the leaving. It is all right.

WALDO
Silent rushes the swift Lord
Through ruined systems still restored,
Broad-sowing, bleak and void to bless,
Plants with worlds the wilderness,
Waters with tears of ancient sorrow

---

[32] *Essay on Experience*, Emerson
[33] *Give All to Love*, poem, Emerson

Apples of Eden ripe to-morrow;
House and tenant go to ground.[34]

ELLEN
Lost in God.[18]

WALDO
In Godhead found.[18]

He returns to the desk.

WALDO
I have wondered from time to time what my last memory will be. After all the others have escaped me. What will be the last? Like Pandora's box, my mind will shut tight, yet one will tap on the lid and cry out "wait! I am still here". Will it be you? Lidian? Henry? Louisa? What will it be? What part of myself will be the last to say goodbye?

ELLEN
It may be a bit selfish but I should like it to be me. But it won't be.

ELLEN
It won't be me.

LIDIAN
Or me.

NELLY
Or me.

LOUISA
Or me.

---

[34] *Threnody*, poem, Emerson

Henry
Or me.

All
For you it will be a boat on river in a land where history waits.

Waldo
I have lived two lives. One of the mind. One of the heart. The mind is leaving. Only the heart remains.

He starts to write.

Waldo
One monument to another.

Fade to Black

The End

Notes

My mother suffered from dementia and resided in a nursing home for the last year or so of her life. I went to visit her most days, and watched as she seemed to travel back through her memories.

First, when she was scared or upset (which was often at first), she would call for me. "Stevie" she would say (which is what my parents always called me). Next she would call for me whether I was there or not, sometimes when I was sitting by her holding her hand. A few months later, she would call for her sister, not Marg, as we referred to her, but "Margaret", which I assume is how she called her as a child. Not long after, she began calling for "Mother", which is how she always referred to my grandmother. Not Mom or Momma but Mother. Finally she stopped calling out at all, as speech left her all together.

As you can imagine, watching this process day after day, and being helpless to do much but sit there and hold her hand and say what few soothing words I could think of, was heart-rending and terrifying. But this is where a little monster lives in all writers. I eventually found a way to use that transformation in my own work, here in this play, as Emerson travels back through his memories.

In July of 1872, Ralph Waldo Emerson's house in Concord, Massachusetts, caught fire. His many friends and admirers raised money for repairs, and to send him on a journey across the ocean while those repairs were being made.

At the time of this voyage, Emerson was one the most famous Americans in the world, and the most famous American intellectual since Franklin. Everywhere he went he was invited to speak and read from his works. But his memory, which had been declining for a few years, declined even more seriously after the fire. No longer considered capable of traveling alone, his daughter Ellen Tucker Emerson (who was named for his first wife) accompanied him and managed the trip.

This tale of a few moments on that voyage is imagined, though based in some details on the letters of Emerson's first wife Ellen and his namesake daughter Ellen, and his journals.

In addition to this episode in Emerson's life, the play travels back to other turning points. First is his relationship with Henry David Thoreau.

In September of 1847, after two productive and life-altering years in his cabin at Walden Pond, Henry David Thoreau left Walden and eventually returned to the household of his friend and mentor Ralph Waldo Emerson.

Why did he leave? In Walden, Thoreau says:

"I left the woods for as good a reason as I went there. Perhaps it seemed to me that I had several more lives to live, and could not spare any more time for that one."

In one section, the play imagines Emerson confronting Thoreau in July 1847, attempting to convince him to leave the cabin at Walden and return to Concord.

A few years earlier, in January 1842, a nine-year-old Louisa May Alcott comes to inquire about Emerson's son Waldo. In January of 1842, Ralph Waldo Emerson's son Waldo fell ill with scarlet fever. Five days later, he died.

As Louisa May Alcott later described that day, her father Bronson, Emerson's close friend, sent his her to see how the young boy was doing. When Emerson opened the door, she explained her errand. "He is dead, child," Emerson said, and slowly closed the door.

This play imagines a different scenario, in which both Emerson's protégé (and jack of all trades) Henry David Thoreau and Emerson's grieving wife Lidian have parts to play.

Louisa from a young age was a frequent visitor to the Emerson household, had looked after the children Waldo and Ellen, and had crushes on the two very different men, both of whom were to influence her life and writing.

Finally, Emerson confronts the loss of his first wife Ellen, who died of consumption only two years after they were married. It is her memory that is his Beatrice, who guides him on the journey through the events of his life.

Emerson, the young Emerson at least, is the most optimistic of philosophers. Yet his life was full of tragedy. He expresses contradictory views of this in two works:

his poem *Threnody*, and his essay *Experience*. Portions of both are included here.

This is the conflict in Emerson that has fascinated and perplexed me for as long as I have been reading him. This play is my attempt at understanding this brilliant, complex, kind, funny, tragic man.

Bibliography

Plutarch:

The Morals, by Plutarch, corrected and revised by William W. Goodwin, Ph. D. 1870

Emerson Biographies:

(My favorites among many)

Emerson: The Mind on Fire by Robert D. Richardson Jr.

Ralph Waldo Emerson by Oliver Wendell Holmes Sr.

Emerson Correspondence:

Letters of Ellen Tucker Emerson, edited by Edith W. Gregg

Letters of Ralph Waldo Emerson, edited by Ralph L. Rusk

One First Love, The Letters of Ellen Luisa Tucker to Ralph Waldo Emerson, edited by Edith W. Gregg

Emerson's Works:

Most of Emerson's own works are in print and/or available online.

Acknowledgements

The original version of Monuments opened as part of the play Generations on August 2, 2019, at Colonial Players in Annapolis, Maryland. The play was directed by Lois Evans and starred Jeffrey Miller and Kate Wheeler.

Generations also included the one-act plays Last Laugh by Morey Norkin and Late Nights in Cars by Michael Gilles.

The first reading of Solid Seasons occurred in Concord, Massachusetts, at the 2023 Thoreau Society Annual Gathering.

I am grateful to the Thoreau Society, which sponsored the event, and to Mr. Brent Ranalli, who offered helpful suggestions, corrected my Thoreau history, and read the part of Henry David Thoreau.

Tourists

Three One-Act Plays

STEPHEN EVANS

A Visitor to Your Planet

Stephen Evans

For the Boatman

Cast of Characters

ALIEN   An alien, who looks like a woman.

MAN   A man, who looks like a man.

Scene

A seashore.

Time

Now.

.

ACT I SCENE 1

Setting: A seashore. There is a boat onstage, turned upside down, bow pointed downstage. It is weathered and a bit battered.

At Rise: The man is painting the boat.

The alien enters and watches him. He doesn't look at her.

ALIEN
I am a visitor to your planet.

MAN
Aren't we all?

She is dismayed by his non-reaction.

ALIEN
I come from another planet.

He still doesn't look at her.

MAN
Welcome.

ALIEN
You believe me?

MAN
I do.

ALIEN
I thought you might be shocked.

MAN
We get a lot of tourists here.

ALIEN
I have carefully chosen this form so as not to frighten you.

The man looks at her for the first time. For a really long time.

MAN
Good choice. Want to sit?

ALIEN
Thank you.

She sits.

ALIEN
What is your name?

MAN
Horatio. What is your name?

ALIEN
Barbie.

MAN
Let me guess. You have carefully chosen that name so as not to frighten me.

ALIEN
How did you know?

MAN
Just guessing. What's your real name?

ALIEN
I cannot pronounce it in this form. Shall I revert to my true form?

He looks at her. Again, for a really long time.

MAN
Barbie will do. There's coffee in that thermos.

She takes the thermos, opens it, looks inside.

ALIEN
What is coffee?

MAN
A consumable liquid foodstuff to sustain energy.

She sniffs.

ALIEN
Ah. Starbucks. One just opened in my galactic sector.

She ours some in a cup and sips.

ALIEN
Nourishing. That is most generous.

MAN
You're welcome.

She sips again.

ALIEN
Aren't you having any?

MAN
Too much caffeine.

ALIEN
Then why do you bring it?

MAN
You don't think you're the first thirsty alien I've met here, do you?

ALIEN
Ahh. Well, it's good.

MAN
Good.

ALIEN
That's what I said.

MAN
No, that was a monosyllabic response of genial acknowledgement. It's a custom round here.

ALIEN
Ahhh.
Pause
Good.

MAN
You'll getting the hang of it.

She stands.

MAN
So I suppose you want me to take you to my leader.

ALIEN
You watch a lot of 1950s science fiction movies, don't you?

MAN
Bugs Bunny cartoons.

ALIEN
Ah yes. I have studied those. They made me a little afraid to contact you.

MAN
Why?

ALIEN
They were so violent. I wondered what kind of intelligent creatures could enjoy such tragic spectacles.

MAN
They are supposed to be funny.

ALIEN
What is funny?

MAN
If I knew the answer to that, I wouldn't be working here.

ALIEN
I don't understand.

MAN
Funny is when you think something hurts but you know it really doesn't.

ALIEN
How can you think something and know something else?

MAN
That's another local custom.

The man continues painting.

ALIEN
Why are you doing that?

MAN
Needs doing.

ALIEN
How do you know?

MAN
It's my work.

ALIEN
What is work?

MAN
What needs doing.

ALIEN
I'm asking you.

MAN
I'm telling you.

ALIEN
What is my work?

MAN
Asking questions?

ALIEN
That is my work!

MAN
You're good at your job.

Long pause

MAN
Is this your first visit to this planet?

ALIEN
Yes. To any planet really. Any other planet. Of course I have been on my planet. I wouldn't want you to think I was planetless.

MAN
You have planetary written all over you. First visit, eh?

ALIEN
Yes.

MAN
Well. We're happy to have you.

ALIEN
Thank you.

MAN
How long have you been here?

ALIEN
One solar revolution.

MAN
A year. That's quite a while for a first visit.

ALIEN
No. One revolution of your solar system around the galaxy. About 230 million of your years.

MAN
I imagine the place has changed a bit.

ALIEN
Yes. For example the last time I stood in this spot it was under the sea.

MAN
Wait a few years and it should look very familiar.

ALIEN
It will.

MAN
Why did you start with this planet?

ALIEN
Each biosphere has a unique rotational signature. About 250 million years ago, the signal from this planet changed drastically, as if your entire world went from shouting to whispering. It was so abrupt–taking less than a million or so years–we felt obligated to investigate. Unfortunately it took about ten million years for the signal to reach us, and then another ten million for me to reach this planet.

MAN
You travel at the speed of light?

ALIEN
In my original form. In this form it would mess up my hair. Plus my mass would increase substantially.

MAN
How does travel increase your mass?

ALIEN
Mass increases with velocity.

MAN
As slowly as I move, you'd think I'd just float away.

ALIEN
Actually you are moving quite rapidly. This planet moves at 28 kilometers per second around your star. This solar system moves at 200 kilometers per second around this little galaxy.

This galaxy moves at 112 kilometers per second towards the next galaxy. And so on.

MAN
I wouldn't worry. Your mass seems just fine.

ALIEN
Thank you.

MAN
Did you ever find out what happened? 250 million years ago?

ALIEN
Yes. Almost all of the life on this planet died.

MAN
I've heard of that. Our scientists call it the Great Extinction.

ALIEN
It is certainly larger than any of the extinctions I have witnessed.

MAN
How many have you seen?

ALIEN
I have been here for four major extinction events. Five if you count the current one.

MAN
The current one?

MAN
Yes, the current extinction event. You are now losing approximately 10,000 species per year. You should reach major extinction levels in just a few centuries. You should be proud of your achievement.

MAN
Why would we be proud? That's terrible.

ALIEN
Oh. I assumed you were doing it on purpose. Your species gives that impression.

MAN
I can see that.

ALIEN
You do seem to be making a noble sacrifice.

MAN
In what way?

ALIEN
Destroying yourselves to save your planet.

MAN
We're doing our best.

ALIEN
It did seem bad planning that you should take so many species with you. But then you are humans; we cannot expect too much.

MAN
I certainly don't. That's one reason I like being out here by myself.

ALIEN
I am disturbing you. Shall I leave?

MAN
No. Please don't. It's not often I get to talk to 230 million year old alien.

ALIEN

Oh I am not 230 million years old.

MAN

I thought you said...

ALIEN

No. I have no age really. Where I am from we have no time. So, no age.

MAN

No time like the present.

ALIEN

Precisely.

He goes on painting.

MAN

So. You've been here a while. What do you think?

ALIEN

About what?

MAN

Our planet. You must have formed some opinions.

ALIEN

I prefer not to think.

MAN

You definitely came to the right place.

ALIEN

I am here merely to observe carefully and bring information back to my civilization.

MAN

I see.

ALIEN
You are the actually first human I have spoken with.

MAN
Really?

ALIEN
It is real.

MAN
How did you manage to be here all this time and not speak to another human?

ALIEN
I was in New York City.

MAN
Ahh.

ALIEN
The shows were good. And the pizza.

MAN
I could be an alien.

ALIEN
You are a human.

MAN
Most of the time.

ALIEN
What are you the rest of the time?

MAN
An animal.

ALIEN
What's the difference?

Long pause. REALLY long.

MAN
Credit cards.

ALIEN
What is a credit card?

MAN
A method of obtaining pizza.

ALIEN
I have seen those. They were long and green.

MAN
No, that's money.

ALIEN
What is money?

MAN
A method of obtaining credit cards.

ALIEN
I see. A credit card is a method of obtaining pizza and money is a method of obtaining a credit card and pizza is a method of obtaining money.

MAN
That's about right.

ALIEN
It seems pointless.

MAN
That's the point. The system is designed to keep us from observing carefully.

ALIEN
I see.

MAN
Do you have credit cards and money where you're from?

ALIEN
No. But then we have no pizza, so we don't need them.

MAN
If you didn't have a credit card, how did you get pizza?

ALIEN
It was difficult at first. But I changed into this form and they seemed quite happy to give it to me.

MAN
For not having spoken to a human, you seem to know our language well.

ALIEN
Thank you. I speak 2,347,691 languages. But only 779, 261 fluently.

MAN
That is a lot.

ALIEN
I have time too. Now.

MAN
I didn't know there were that many languages.

ALIEN
All substances have language. Quartz is my favorite. It is simple and pure. Willow is very complex.

MAN
And sad?

ALIEN
Yes. Do you speak willow?

MAN
I speak sad.

ALIEN
Most languages are simpler than yours. Your language causes me great difficulty.

MAN
Why?

ALIEN
It changes so much.

MAN
Your language doesn't change?

ALIEN
Never. But then we don't have words.

MAN
How can you have a language without words?

ALIEN
Once we had words. But they just seem to confuse everyone.

MAN
So do you communicate telepathically? Mind to mind.

ALIEN
No. We have one word that means everything and never ends. And we each speak our part of it.

MAN
Conversation must be difficult.

ALIEN
It is impossible.

MAN
I think I might like your world.

Pause.

MAN
So how did you happen to pick me to speak to?

ALIEN
You were alone.

MAN
Can't argue with that.

ALIEN
You seemed to have some time.

MAN
Can't argue with that either. Time I have.

ALIEN
Do you wish to?

MAN
Have time? No one has ever asked me that. I suppose I do. Not much that I would rather have than time, come to think of it.

ALIEN
No. I mean. Do you wish to argue?

MAN
Oh. Hmm. Not really.

ALIEN

I would argue with you if you wish. I have never argued with a human before.

MAN

That's thoughtful of you. But no.

ALIEN

There was something your voice, as if you missed arguing.

He pauses.

MAN

I don't miss arguing. I suppose. I suppose sometimes I miss the person I used to argue with.

ALIEN

I see. Then arguing is a beneficial ritual between humans.

MAN

It can be. In the right circumstances it leads to making up.

ALIEN

Ah. We could argue and then make up. If you like.

MAN

I don't think we know each other well enough. But as we say, time will tell.

ALIEN

Who is we? Is this your social concatenation?

MAN

I never did know who we was. And I'm not sure I think too much of we anyway.

ALIEN

Then let us not speak of we if we do not please you.

The man gets up, stands back, and observes his work. The alien stands back with him and does the same. He nods. She nods too. The man goes back and paints for a while.

ALIEN
What is this work?

MAN
I'm painting my boat.

ALIEN
Why do you do that?

MAN
Needs doing.

ALIEN
I would be pleased to not have that discussion again.

MAN
You are very polite for an alien.

ALIEN
Are not most aliens polite?

MAN
They are not impolite. But most of the time they don't talk to me. They just sit and watch the sunrise or sunset.

ALIEN
Yes. You are very lucky on this planet. Most planets do not have such colorful displays. Either the atmosphere is too thin and there is simply a flood of light morning and evening. Or the atmosphere is too thick and the light cannot get through at all. Or the planet is too close to the star and the light and heat are too intense, or too far and they are barely noticeable.

MAN
I guess we are lucky.

ALIEN
And this.
She points to the sea.
99.999 percent of the water in the universe is either frozen or gas. There is more liquid water on this planet than in all the rest of your galaxy combined.

MAN
I didn't know that.

ALIEN
This was a remarkable world.

MAN
Was? We still have the sea. We still have sunsets.

ALIEN
True. But soon you will not be around to enjoy them.

MAN
Point taken. What is your planet like?

ALIEN
There are not words in your language to describe it.

MAN
Ahh.

ALIEN
I could tell you in quartz.

MAN
When are you going home?

ALIEN
I don't know for sure. They were supposed to come pick me up 229 million years ago.

MAN
I'm sure they'll be here any minute.

She looks up.

ALIEN
It cannot be ruled out. But it is unlikely. We don't have minutes.

MAN
No minutes?

She shakes her head.

MAN
Days?

She shakes her head.

MAN
Solar revolutions?

ALIEN
No. As I said, we have no time. We have only now.

MAN
We have only have now here ourselves. We just like to pretend about days and minutes.

ALIEN
And solar revolutions.

MAN
Those too.

ALIEN
I guess it is 230 million years for me and now for them. Possibly this was a flaw in our planning.

MAN
Happens to the best of us.

Long pause.

MAN
Will you miss this planet when you go?

ALIEN
I will. I will miss the changingness. Is that a word?

MAN
It is now.

ALIEN
Will you?

MAN
Will I?

ALIEN
Will you miss this planet when you go?

MAN
A minute ago, I would have said yes.

ALIEN
Can so much change in a minute?

MAN
Not really. But now can change everything. As the willow would say.

ALIEN
True.

MAN
What if they never come for you? Will you die?

She points at him.

ALIEN
E.T. Great film.

MAN
Will you?

ALIEN
My people do not die. That is one reason I came. We do not understand why you would choose to die.

MAN
We don't choose to die. That's just life. You are born and you die.

ALIEN
This is the only planet in the universe where living beings die.

MAN
There is no death anywhere else?

ALIEN
No.

MAN
Huh. It never occurred to me there was any other option. I just thought that is what life was, everywhere. We come and we go.

ALIEN
I have watched countless creatures die in my time here. Whole species. Whole collections of species. I have observed most carefully each time, trying to understand the reason. But after 230 million years, I still do not understand.

MAN
Do you have religion on your planet?

ALIEN
Religion. You mean pre-determined rituals for communing with imaginary beings?

MAN
No. That would be marriage. I mean worship of a divine order.

ALIEN
There is no order in the universe. I thought humans knew that.

MAN
Why would you think that?

ALIEN
You act that way.

MAN
Fair point.

ALIEN
There cannot be order where there is no multiplicity. All only is, or can ever be.

MAN
Amen.

ALIEN
On my planet we worship no order, divine or otherwise.

MAN
Then how do you maintain a society?

ALIEN
We're just nice.

MAN
I see. So you don't have time and you don't have death and you don't have religion.

ALIEN
No.

MAN
Then you don't have an afterlife?

ALIEN
Afterlife?

MAN
A transition to a better place after death.

ALIEN
No we have no such thing. Do you?

MAN
It's one of those things we think but know something else. No death anywhere else. I wonder why we have death?

ALIEN
I do have one possible guess. But you must not tell anyone. I am not supposed to draw conclusions.

MAN
Don't worry. I'll be dead soon.

ALIEN
True.

MAN
So what is your guess?

ALIEN
It is the changingness. No other world has death, and no other world has the changingness. One is the price of the other.

MAN
Death is the price of change?

ALIEN
No. Change is the price of death. There is so much death here. It must be a good thing. Perhaps it is this afterlife. Perhaps the afterlife is something you know but do not think.

MAN
I suppose I'll find out soon enough.

ALIEN
Not if you come with me.

MAN
Come with you?

ALIEN
You could come with me.

MAN
I could?

ALIEN
I offer you a part of my word. That is a beneficial ritual where I come from.

MAN
I would live forever?

ALIEN
You would live now.

MAN
So if you can't die, what do you do?

ALIEN
Mostly we remember.

MAN
Remember. What will you remember about this planet?

Long pause.

ALIEN
Pizza.

MAN
I can see that.

ALIEN
And sunsets. And seashores. And you.

MAN
I would like to be remembered. You know, I think I would like to be remembered more than I would like to remember.

ALIEN
We all have our work.

He paints the last brushstroke.

MAN
Done.

ALIEN
You are finished?

MAN
Almost. I just need a name.

ALIEN
You have a name.

MAN
No. I need a name for my boat.

ALIEN
I don't suppose boats frighten you.

MAN
No.

ALIEN
So you would not need to carefully chose the name so as not to frighten yourself.

MAN
No.

ALIEN
Then how do you choose a name?

MAN
That is a good question. The name of a boat is very important. Your boat keeps you alive. It keeps you fed. It keeps you free. A boat is a unique and special creature. And the name has to reflect that.

ALIEN
You have chosen a name, haven't you?

MAN
I have.

He paints the name Barbie.

ALIEN
That is my name.

MAN
It is.

ALIEN
You won't get confused?

MAN
I may. But I'm used to it. It is my natural state as a human.

ALIEN
You painted it upside down. Perhaps that will help you tell us apart.

MAN
I painted it right-side up. It is the boat that is upside down.

ALIEN
I am relieved. It seemed a flaw in your planning. But I didn't wish to mention it.

MAN
Thank you.

The man stands back again and observes his work. The alien stands back with him and does the same. He nods. She nods too.

MAN
Okay then.

ALIEN
So now you have finished your work.

MAN
Yes.

ALIEN
Then let us go.

MAN
Where?

ALIEN
Where do you think?

They look up. Then look at each other.

TOGETHER
Pizza!

They start to leave. The lights start to fade.

ALIEN
Do you have a credit card?

Blackout

The End

STEPHEN EVANS

Arc

Cast of Characters

GWEN   A Grace Kelly look-alike (more the actress than the princess despite her 60 years)

ART   Gwen's age, a writer, more William Powell than Robert Redford.

MERLE The station vendor, who looks a little bit like the Princeton version of Einstein (sweatshirt and sneakers included).

Scene:

A train station.

Time:

Who knows?

.

Act I Scene 1

Setting: A small train station. A few old benches are crowded together in the center. On the upstage wall is a round clock, the numbers, roman numerals, barely visible through the round crystal face, have delicate green vines climbing up them, twining around them. The time says 11:55 through most of the play. Upstage under the clock is a door to the train platform, with two old wooden chairs beneath. To the side is a cart for a vendor that offers newspapers, coffee, and various treats.

At Rise: MERLE sits doing a crossword puzzle behind the vendor cart. GWEN is the only other occupant of the station. She sits on the front bench, glancing occasionally back at the clock.

MERLE
Hey. Hey Lady.

Gwen turns around.

MERLE
What's an eight-letter word for unusual? Starts with a U. Not unusual. Well, unusual does. But unusual but not unusual. If you get me.

GWEN
Unwonted.

He counts it out.

MERLE
No, this one has an o in it.

GWEN
Unw*o*nted.

MERLE
Ah. Unwanted. Got ya.

He counts it out again.

MERLE
How do you spell that?

GWEN
(Spelling it out).
U-N-W-O-N-T-E-D. As in unwonted silence.

MERLE
Ah. Unwonted. Got ya. Thanks.

She smiles and turns back. He goes back to his crossword.

MERLE
Hey Lady.

Gwen turns around again.

MERLE
When's your train?

GWEN
Soon.

She smiles and turns back.

GWEN

I hope.

MERLE

Want some coffee. On the house. Not much busy tonight.

Gwen turns around again.

GWEN

I'm not a coffee drinker. But thanks.

She smiles and turns back. He goes back to his crossword.

MERLE

Snickers? Chips. I got chips. Gum. Cigarettes. Except you can't smoke in here.

Gwen turns around again.

MERLE

Used to. Used to you could smoke. Some days you could hardly breathe. I been here thirty-four years, right in this booth. Well, I mean I go home. But I've been working here thirty-four years. I inherited from my uncle. He was here twenty-seven years, right when they opened this place.

GWEN

I imagine things have changed in thirty-four years.

MERLE

You'd think so, wouldn't you?

She smiles and turns back. He goes back to his crossword.

                    MERLE
Hey lady?

> *Gwen turns around again.*

                    GWEN
Mints. I'd like some mints.

> *Merle beams. He lives for this.*

                    MERLE
Stay there. I'll bring.

> *He walks down, hands her some mints, and sits. Gwen opens the package, takes one.*

                    MERLE
I'm Merle.

                    GWEN
Gwen.

                    MERLE
Thirty-four years I've worked here. Seven more than my uncle. Beat him by seven. But only because he died. So I don't brag about it.

                    GWEN
Mint?

                    MERLE
Sure. Thanks. Thirty-four years. I could have retired. But what? I do the crossword at home? Where is the sense in that?

> *He looks at her. After a second, she nods.*

MERLE
Speaking of. I better get back to it. I like to finish it by the time I leave.

GWEN
Good for you. I never finished one in my life.

Merle shrugs.

MERLE
If you don't stop, eventually you finish. You have a good trip.

GWEN
Thank you.

He gets up and goes back to his cart. She spits out the mint.

ART walks through the door. When he sees Gwen, he stops, waiting a long time, before deciding to go in. He rounds into her view, and waves. She smiles, waves back. He walks down to her.

GWEN
I didn't know if.

ART
Are you kidding? It's not often I get an invitation from the past.

He gestures to the bench.

GWEN
Really? I get them all the time.

He gestures to the bench. She nods. He sits.

ART
I was surprised to get your call.

GWEN
I was surprised you had the same phone number.

ART
Some things don't change.

GWEN
Most things do. Until they change back.

ART
So. What brings you back here?

GWEN
The funeral.

ART
Not your Dad?

GWEN
No. He's still.

ART
I can imagine. I mean. Good for him. He must be…

GWEN
93 last January.

They pause.

ART
So. Whose funeral?

GWEN
Izzy.

ART

Izzy. Who?

GWEN

She was in our class Senior year.

ART

Can't place her.

GWEN

She wasn't in our crowd.

ART

Ah. Did we have a crowd?

GWEN

More of gang. Gaggle. Pandemonium. Quiver.

ART

Quiver?

GWEN

Cobras.

ART

Ah. That's about right.

Another pause.

ART

I want to ask how the funeral was. But it sort of answers itself.

GWEN

A lot of people there. I thought I might see you.

ART

Didn't hear about it.

GWEN
I think they should have funerals before you die. It seems rude to wait.

ART
It does, doesn't it?

GWEN
The nicest party you're ever invited to, and you really can't enjoy it.

ART
Weddings are nice. So I hear.

GWEN
You never?

He shakes his head.

ART
You?

GWEN
Twice. No. Three times. Depends on how you count.

ART
Does it?

GWEN
You and Izzy should have gotten together. I mean you live in the same small town. You'd think your paths would have crossed.

ART
I'm not much of a path-crosser. How about you?

GWEN
No. Except at funerals. And train stations.

ART
Is that why we're meeting here? You know you have a getaway scheduled?

GWEN
Maybe. And maybe I didn't want to spend my last minutes in this town with Merle.

ART
Who?

GWEN
Mint?

ART
Uh. Sure.

Gwen looks back.

GWEN
Hey Merle.

MERLE
Yes, Milady?

GWEN
You have any coffee left? We could both use a cup.

MERLE
Sure.

He pulls out a carafe.

ART
You always had a penchant for making friends.

GWEN
You always had a penchant for saying words like penchant.

She pulls a book out of her carry-on bag.

GWEN
I finished your last book.

ART
Ah. You were the one who bought it.

GWEN
It reminded me of you.

ART
Hopefully that's a compliment.

GWEN
A not uncomplicated one, but yes.

ART
That's fair to say.

GWEN
It seemed like one of the characters might have been based on me.

ART
Maybe. In a not uncomplicated way.

GWEN
We had a not uncomplicated time together.

ART
We're not uncomplicated people.

GWEN
Would you sign it for me?

ART
Sure. Do you have a pen?

GWEN
Oh.

She starts to search through her bag.

ART
Don't worry. I have one.

He pulls out a pen.

GWEN
Then why did you ask?

ART
In Author school, we're taught not to seem too eager. It's an image thing.

He signs it and hands it back. She reads it and laughs.

GWEN
To not uncomplicated memories. Funny.

ART
They teach us that too. And how to look humble.

GWEN
Your handwriting has not improved.

ART
That they could not teach.

She puts the book away, burying it in her bag like treasure.

GWEN
I kept your letters.

                        ART
From when we were together or from when we weren't.

                        GWEN
Both.

                        ART
I'm surprised they haven't turned to dust. Or been remaindered.

                        GWEN
Are you saying we're old and unwanted?

> *Merle arrives behind them, bearing two light blue paper cups of coffee with dark plastic lids.*

                        MERLE
U-N-W-O-N-T-E-D. As in unwonted silence. See I remember things.

> *He hands each of them a cup. Art glances at Gwen.*

                        GWEN
Crossword. Thank you, Merle.

> *Merle draws packets of sweetener and creamer out of seemingly every pocket and dumps a bunch onto the bench between them.*

                        MERLE
Sorry. It's been sitting a while.

                        GWEN
So have I.

                        MERLE
I can brew new!

Gwen and Art
If only.

They smile.

Gwen
This is fine. We just need something to cover the unwonted silences.

Merle looks one to the other, and likes what he sees.

Merle
Actually I don't brew myself. I get from the coffee shop next door. It's good. So I'll go borrow. You'll watch my cart?

Gwen
Like two hawks.

He exits.

Art
Are you expecting any?

Gwen
Coffee?

Art
Unwonted silences.

Gwen
No, just the wonted ones.

They look at each other for a while. She takes a drink. He does too. They both add lots more cream and sugar.

Art
Well I'm glad we got that out of the way.

GWEN
Me too.

He stands.

ART
Walk?

GWEN
I still get around.

He smiles.

ART
Would you like to take a walk?

GWEN
I would. But. My train should be here soon.

She glances at the clock.

GWEN
That's the theory anyway.

He glances at the clock, then at her, then back at the clock, then at his phone.

GWEN
I think maybe it's the Doomsday clock. It hasn't moved since I've been here, fortunately.

ART
Even a broken clock is right twice a day.

GWEN
Actually a stopped clock is right twice a day. A broken clock may never be right.

####### ART
True. Well, since we aren't facing imminent Armageddon, how about a walk just around the station?

####### GWEN
Take a turn around the room? How Jane Austen of you.

####### ART
I'm nervous.

####### GWEN
Why?

####### ART
I haven't been up this late in about 30 years.

She stands.

####### GWEN
There is that. A turn it is. Shall we go armed?

She picks up the coffee cups, hands his to him, then looks around her at the station.

####### GWEN
Clockwise or counterclockwise?

He glances at the clock.

####### ART
With this clock, I'm not sure there is a difference.

####### GWEN
Good point. Left or right. Sunside or widdershins? Upstream or downstream?

####### ART
Upstream. It's more literary.

                    GWEN
Born back ceaselessly into the past.

> *She slips her free arm in his and begins to stroll. He matches her stride instinctively.*

                    ART
Are you going far?

                    GWEN
Just once around.

                    ART
Are you traveling far?

                    GWEN
You also had a penchant for existential questions.

                    ART
I meant your train. Not prying. Just wondering.

> *Gwen laughs.*

                    GWEN
You had a penchant for that too

                    ART
Wondering where you live now.

> *They reach the end of the row of benches. She stops and takes a sip of coffee. He does too. She is getting used to the taste. He isn't, but he drinks anyway, keeping pace. Then they rotate in concert.*

                    GWEN
I'm between homes at the moment.

> *Art stops, puts his hand on her arm.*

ART

You're homeless?

She shakes her head.

GWEN

No. I have five. I just don't know which to go to.

Art pauses.

ART

Five homes. Why do you have five homes?

Gwen shrugs.

GWEN

Two and a half husbands times two.

Art does the math in his head, never his strong point. But it seems right.

ART

You know you can sell them. You don't have to keep them forever.

Gwen pauses. They are at the point in a meeting of old friends where some account of the years is required, and she is not sure that at whatever time at night it is that she has the energy. But she can see that he will not accept the short answer. She sighs.

GWEN

I hold onto them as, as a reminder of what I should never do again.

Art sits back, looks away, then back at her.

ART

That bad?

GWEN

Not in the living. Only in the remembering.

Arts nods. Then shakes his head. Then nods. She wonders what mental process stimulated that sequence.

ART

I hate that, he concludes at the end of the tortuous mental algorithm.

GWEN

You too?

Art grimaces a bit, realizing himself that they have entered another and likely uncomfortable phase of revelation.

ART

Sort of. I'll write something. And in the moment, I'll be convinced that is it the most brilliant thing I have ever written. Then I'll read it again later, a year if I'm brave, five if I'm not.

GWEN

Not as good?

Never

GWEN

Not even once?

ART

Not even.

                          GWEN
How odd.

> *They pause to be sure. They laugh. A sly look crosses over his face.*

                          ART
Do you mind?

                          GWEN
I can't seem to help it.'

> *Art smiles.*

                          ART
I don't want to pry.

                          GWEN
I invited you. It's my own fault.

                          ART
I'm just curious. Never having.

> *They reach the end of the next row of benches. She stops and takes a sip of coffee. He does too. She is getting used to the taste. He isn't, but he drinks anyway, keeping pace. Then they rotate in concert.*

                          GWEN
I understand. Ask.

                          ART
Divorced?

                          GWEN
One divorce, one widowing, one annulment.

ART
Annulment. They still do that?

GWEN
So my lawyer says.

ART
Why?

GWEN
He had another wife he forgot to mention.

ART
Ah. That's significant.

GWEN
Yes. It's not the good kind of threesome.

He stops a moment, processing, trying not to imagine.

ART
I'm starting to feel a bit provincial here.

Gwen smiles.

GWEN
Small town. And it's charming.

ART
Really?

At the end of the last row of benches, Gwen stops and laughs.

GWEN
Don't tell me you don't know.

ART
I could never tell with you, how you felt about things.

She lifts her hand, rescues him from some lint.

GWEN
I thought I made my feelings pretty clear. A number of times.

ART
Well. That. Yes.

Gwen restarts the stroll.

GWEN
I sometimes wonder. If. Back then. If you had asked me to marry you—

He pauses, then follows slightly behind her.

ART
I did.

GWEN
You might have saved me two and a half marriages and five houses I don't like.

ART
I did ask.

GWEN
Or maybe it would be three and a half marriages and seven houses. Who knows?

ART
I did ask.

GWEN
Life takes these funny turns. Except I never seem to laugh.

ART
Gwen. I did ask.

She stops underneath the recalcitrant clock, and notices the clock face reflected in the darkened windows throughout the station, though the wall on which it hangs is not itself visible in the reflection, so the clock appears suspended in the air. Some trick, of the hanging lights (which lights themselves are also suspended in the dark like stars around the moon) reflecting off the clock face or the wind outside against the ancient windows or just her own tired vision, makes it seem as if the hands of the mirrored clock are turning now, but backwards. She tries to work out whether a clock in a mirror would go retrograde, working out the vectors of reflection.

She steps out a pace and glances up at the actual clock. He joins her, looks up, sees the motionless clock, gives her a questioning glance. She steps back against the wall, tilts her head and squints a bit and the illusion in the mirror resolves; the hands once more are still.

ART

What?

GWEN

For a minute, as I was watching the clock's reflection in the windows, I thought it was moving.

Then his words finally register. She looks at him as he stands in front of her, amusement now replacing his confusion.

GWEN

You did what?

Art nods.

                    ART
I did ask. You to marry me.

Long pause. They both take a sip of coffee.

Gwen looks around. There are two ancient wooden chairs to the left of the track door. She sits, sending her memory on a quest.

                    GWEN
Are you sure?

He laughs, sits in the other chair.

                    ART
I'm positive.

Now it is Gwen's head that twists, one way, then, the other.

                    GWEN
Were we stoned? It doesn't count if you're stoned.

                    ART
We were not. It counted for me. The one and only.

She looks at him.

                    GWEN
No.

He nods his head.

                    GWEN
You're not joking?

                    ART
No.

GWEN
And it wasn't a joke then? That we maybe just laughed off.

ART
I did not laugh it off.

GWEN
Because we were only?'

ART
I was 21. You were.

GWEN
(Quickly)
Younger. Huh. Really? Wow. Maybe I didn't like you as much as I remember.

ART
Apparently.

Gwen sips. He still does not.

GWEN
Was I nice about it at least?

Art's lips come together, as he tries to decide how to characterize the moment. Then he nods.

ART
You were. Sort of.

He turns his body to her.

ART
You pretended it didn't happen. Went on talking about going to Europe for the summer.

GWEN
Really? I said nothing?

He slides his hand along the back of her chair.

ART
Not about that. You started talking about how you heard Prague was so beautiful and you couldn't wait to see the Volga.

GWEN
Vltava.

ART
Gesundheit.

GWEN
Funny. The Vltava flows through Prague.

ART
I didn't know that then.

GWEN
Probably neither did I.

Art crosses his arms over his chest.

ART
So we finished our dinner and I took you home.

Gwen is still lost in the struggle to recall any of the episode. Finally.

GWEN
Did we break up?

ART
Not till you went to Europe that summer.

She turns to him, with pseudo-anger to cover a growing and unexpected sense of remorse.

GWEN
A woman turns down your proposal of marriage and you still date her? What, have you no self-respect?

Art shrugs.

ART
The sex was really good.

Gwen stares at him, then shrugs herself, turning back and leaning against the slatted back of the chair, her head resting against the ancient wall.

GWEN
Oh. Well. Sure. You're a man. Wait. Where did this alleged proposal take place?

ART
Jake's Crab House.

Gwen laughs. Loudly. Merle glances, returns to his crossword smiling.

GWEN
What? Did you want me to say no?

Now Art glares.

Of course not.

GWEN
Did you want me to say yes?

ART
Probably. I doubt that I thought through the alternatives.

Gwen shrugs again.

GWEN
Oh. Well. Sure. You're a man. So you proposed to me at the noisiest restaurant on the East Coast. Did you get down on one knee?

ART
No. It was a crab house. The floor was a mess.

GWEN
Understandable. Was there a ring?

ART
There was, but I never got to that part.

Gwen hums a bit, pondering.

GWEN
So I have a theory.

ART
Don't say it.

GWEN
You know what it is?

ART
I think so.

Gwen spins her body toward him again, and reaches out her non-coffee hand to touch his cheek. Then slaps him slightly. Just the merest touch.

ART
I don't think I heard you.

He closes his eyes. He has thought about that moment many times over the years, coming to the same conclusion.

ART
I don't think you did either.

Long pause. They both take a sip, leaning back into the wall. But the coffee is gone. Art takes the cups, walks to a trash can, deposits, returns, and sits.

Gwen twists and slides closer to him, with her back resting against his shoulder.

GWEN
Wow.

ART
I know.

GWEN
I mean.

ART
I know!

GWEN
Wow.

ART
I know.

Gwen revolves and looks into his eyes, so curious to see what she can see there. Mostly, there is humor. Then deeper, wonder at the questions of the evening: what if? And behind that, understanding, that they have had their paths, and that those paths have brought them here. And somehow here in the station beneath the stopped or broken clock the question in both their minds is transformed, from what if?, to what now? And they both realize that, but neither knows how to face it, or answer it.

GWEN
Can you imagine? she says.

ART
Vividly. Every day. For several years.

Gwen reaches up, patting his cheek again, nicely this time.

GWEN
Poor boy.

ART
I had even spoken to your father beforehand.

GWEN
No!

ART
Yep. In my 20-year-old classic nerd mind, it was the right thing to do.

GWEN
What did my father say?

Art smiles.

ART
He said, good luck. In that way he had of saying, no way in hell but I respect you for asking anyway.

GWEN
Yes. He could say a lot in a few words. Can say.

ART
He never told you about it?

GWEN
Never told, never asked.

Gwen takes his hand.

GWEN
I mean. Our whole lives. Could have been. Our whole lives.

ART
Yes. Maybe. Who knows?

Gwen laughs, sighs, laughs again.

GWEN
It's mind boggling.

ART
It is.

GWEN
So.

ART
Yes?

GWEN
How long have you held this theory that I never heard you?

ART
Since the next day.

GWEN
That's a long time.

ART
Almost—

GWEN
Oh let's not.

ART
Agreed.

Gwen works her way through vague memories of the evening.

GWEN
Why didn't you say anything?

Now Art laughs loudly. In the empty station it reverberates, almost an echo but not quite—more a remembrance of laughter lost.

ART
What was I supposed to say? Oh by the way, did you hear my proposal of marriage?

GWEN
I see the problem.

ART
I did not want to go through it again.

GWEN
Even though you may not have gone through it the first time?

ART
I went through it. Apparently you didn't.

GWEN
I suppose.

He crosses his arms over his chest.

ART
It was the most soul-crushing experience of my entire life. I was devastated. You know. At that age. How you feel things.

Gwen performs her sort-of chuckle again, and leans her head against his shoulder.

GWEN
That I remember. I'm so sorry.

He sighs.

ART
Thank you. Though.

She raises up, looks at him.

GWEN
Yes?

ART
I am curious. I suppose that's why I came.

GWEN
Is it? Then ask.

ART
Now I'm not sure I want to know. Is it worth knowing, while knowing that it changes nothing?

She thinks.

GWEN
It changes nothing that has happened. But you don't know that it would change nothing in the future. Or even the now.

ART
Now that is existential. You must have learned it from me.

GWEN
Possibly.

He turns to her and takes her hand.

GWEN
You're not going to propose again are you?

ART
No. Are you disappointed?

GWEN
Possibly. I've had several, but I am curious how you would go about it.

ART
Not well, apparently. Considering.

GWEN
True. But perhaps you learned something from the first attempt.

ART
I don't think this is something where experience is a help.

GWEN
True. It didn't help me, I can say that. So if you're not proposing, what do you want to know?

He pauses, decides to go ahead and ask.

ART
If you had heard?

                    GWEN
Yes?

> *Art draws out the sentence.*

                    ART
What do you think you would have said?

> *Gwen hesitates.*

                    GWEN
Mint?

> *Art mock scowls.*

                    ART
Oh come on. I've waited mphmfh years for an answer.

> *She shakes her head.*

                    GWEN
How could I possibly know now what I would have felt then if?

                    ART
I know how I felt.

                    GWEN
How?

                    ART
I felt that no one else in the world could wear a baseball cap as well as you. I felt that when you jogged by my house in the morning with your ponytail swinging side to side that the earth spun a little slower just to give me more time to gaze at you in wonder. I felt that when you shook your hair a certain way there was air to breathe. I felt that when my arms were

around you I didn't need the air anymore and when your hand was in mine my heart didn't need to beat. I felt that flowers leaned your way when you passed and the grass turned greener just for you. I felt that your silhouette just filled the empty space in my life like one of those cartoon cutouts. I felt that when you smiled a butterfly must be born somewhere because that much beauty must have consequences.

GWEN
That's how you felt?

ART
Yes.

GWEN
Was that how you proposed?

ART
No. I think when I proposed I said something like: I think we should get married. Don't you?

GWEN
That's what you said?

He can't look at her. He wonders if he will ever be able to look at her again, and then wonders if after tonight he will ever get another chance.

There may have been an extra pause or two, but pretty much.

GWEN
But that other, the baseball cap and the running.

ART
Jogging

                    GWEN
And the grass and the butterfly. You remember all that.

                    ART
I do.

                    GWEN
How?

                    ART
I wrote it down.

> *He takes out his wallet and unfolds a ragged piece of paper.*

First bit of writing I ever did.

> *She reaches for it. He doesn't let it go at first, but finally he does. She stares at the unfolded paper*

                    GWEN
And you kept it. All this time.

                    ART
Sort of.

                    GWEN
What do you mean—sort of?

> *Art takes it back. She doesn't want to let it go, but she does.*

                    ART
Well. I look at it once in a while.

                    GWEN
You look at it.

ART

After a few years it wears out. So I retype it. I still have my old typewriter and I found some of the same notepaper. So it looks the same.

Gwen reaches for the paper, but he doesn't give it to her.

GWEN

How many times have you retyped it?

ART

I don't know.

ART

Give me a ballpark number.

Art sighs again.

ART

This is eight.

GWEN

Eight.

ART

Eight.

GWEN

So did you keep it because it was your first real piece of writing or because it reminded you of how you felt about me.

ART

The first one.

GWEN

Oh.

ART
I didn't need anything to remind me how I felt about you. And then I didn't want anything to remind me. And then it didn't remind me. Because I found I had it memorized.

ART
Would you?

GWEN
Marry you? I heard that one.

ART
Like to have it?

GWEN
You don't want it anymore?

ART
I put it in a book. It's what we authors do.

GWEN
Ah. Okay. Thanks. I would like to have it. Might be worth something someday, the first piece of writing by a famous novelist that he used in his best-known novel.

ART
You saw that?

GWEN
I told you I read it.

ART
I never assume my work is memorable.

> *There is a long pause. They both feel the energy has ebbed a bit, and the disappointment has is seeping in in its place.*

Merle enters. They don't notice. He watches for a moment. Then bustles up, carafe in one hand, fresh cups in the other.

MERLE
Looks like I'm just in time.

He hands each of them a round clear mug like a glass ball with the top open, then pours the liquid carefully into Gwen's cup.

MERLE
Coffee, fresh.

He pours into Art's cup.

MERLE
There. Now you're ready for another unwonted silence.

GWEN
You're really liking that word, aren't you?

Merle again unloads handfuls of creamer and sugar packets onto the bench.

MERLE
Why do you think I do crosswords?

More sugar.

MERLE
You're never too old.

More creamer.

MERLE
Well, that's not true. Sometimes you are.

More multi-colored packs of sweetener.

MERLE
But you're never too old to think you're never too old. And that's the truth.

Gwen smiles at him, genuine, and amused.

GWEN
Thank you, Merle.

Merle assumes a mission accomplished pose.

MERLE
It's what I'm here for.

ART
Yes, thank you. Our silences are now covered for the remainder of the evening. Morning. Whichever time this is.

Merle unposes, goes back to his cart. Gwen and Art look at each other for a moment. They take a long sip without losing eye contact, then simultaneous smiles of delight. Neither adds anything extra to the cup. Gwen swivels.

GWEN
This is delicious. Thank you Merle. Just what we needed.

Merles waves away the praise. Art stands, holds out his hand to Gwen.

ART
Shall we?

She takes his hand and stands.

GWEN
We shall.

They continue to the end of the first row of benches, passing Merle's cart. Merle has returned to his crossword, diligently chanting the words to himself.

Gwen and Art make it down the aisle about halfway, when Gwen glances back at Merle, then sighs.

GWEN
Must be nice.

ART
What?

GWEN
To know what you're here for.

ART
You're here for a funeral.

Gwen catches his eye again, looks intently for a moment, then sighs again.

GWEN
Am I?

ART
Aren't you?

GWEN
I suppose. A funeral. A commemoration of loss and passage.

She turns around.

GWEN
Hey Merle, what's another word for funeral?

MERLE
(*Without looking up*)
Exequy.

Gwen is impressed.

GWEN
How about a word for funeral song?

MERLE
(*Still without looking up*)
Epicedium.

Gwen nods.

GWEN
Yes. That's why I'm here. I'm here for an epicedium.

MERLE
(*Still without looking up*)
Your crossword is depressing.

Gwen nods.

GWEN
It is, isn't it?

ART
You're in a pensive mood.

GWEN
Is that the right word? Pensive?

ART
It must be. I'm a writer.

GWEN
Then I guess I am.

GWEN
No. I wouldn't say pensive.

ART
What would you call it?

GWEN
I don't think I'd call it anything.

ART
I see.

At the final turn, they swing around towards the place where they began, marked by the bag and the book. They take the few short steps in silence, pondering.

GWEN
If I call my mood something, it will send it off in one direction or another. And this mood is something that needs go where it's going and I need to wait until it gets there. Like my train.

Having reached her seat, Gwen hesitates.

ART
Would you like me to wait with you?

Art drains the last of his coffee. Gwen looks at him intently, and if he didn't know better he would have said she was sticking her tongue out at him. But he did know better.

GWEN
As it turns out.

She drinks the last of her own coffee. He downs his.

GWEN
As it turns out, I would like that very much.

She puts her hand on his. He smiles. They sit in their original places, eyes never straying during the descent, and set their empty cups to the side.

ART
Why the train? Just curious.

GWEN
I always travel by train.

ART
Why?

GWEN
Why? I don't know. I like the getting there. Instead of just the arriving.

Art nods.

ART
I like the train too.

GWEN
Really? Why?

ART
They travel in lines. No arcs. No parabolas through the sky. No short cuts across the earth. Here to there. I'm a here-to-there kind of guy.

GWEN
You always were.

ART
Was I? I don't think of myself that way.

She shakes her head.

GWEN
You always were. Trust me.

Art says nothing for a moment.

ART
How about you?

GWEN
Here to there? Not so much.

She takes a sip.

GWEN
Or. I don't know. Maybe. In a not uncomplicated way.

ART
I meant. Are you what you always were?

GWEN
What do you think?

Art laughs. She likes this laugh, deep and genuine.

ART
With you? I think there is no past tense.

GWEN
More likely subjunctive.

ART
If only that were true.

Gwen laughs, then frowns at him.

                    GWEN
You're a writer. It's your job to know these things.

> *Art laughs. They have a rhythm going. Then he sighs.*

                    ART
The more I write, the more I think my job is not to know anything.

                    GWEN
Stop writing.

                    ART
Now there, past tense is appropriate.

> *Gwen puts her hand on his forearm and pulls him around to her.*

                    GWEN
You can't stop writing.

                    ART
Why not?

                    GWEN
How will we know what happens next?

> *Art pats her hand, slips his fingers under it and holds it.*

                    ART
Maybe nothing will.

> *She kisses him.*

                    GWEN
You never know.

> *He nods.*

ART

You never do.

GWEN

So you don't like past tense and you don't like subjunctive and you don't like future tense. What will you write?

ART

Screenplays.

She thinks.

GWEN

I could see that.

ART

Conditional. Wouldn't that be nice.

He stops, turns to her.

ART

Are you okay?

Gwen takes her time in answering, both to decide what to tell, and to decide what the answer is. It is such a simple question—and like most such questions it does not have a simple answer.

GWEN

I'm alive.

ART

Is that an answer?

GWEN

It's the only answer I know.

Art pauses, wondering if he should pursue it, wondering if he has the right to know more, wondering if she is right that it is the only answer.

ART
Okay, what shall we do while we wait?

Gwen pauses, realizing that their conversation has now become punctuated by time.

GWEN
Let's talk about you.

ART
Me? That is a very short story. I hope you don't have long to wait.

Gwen smiles.

GWEN
According to the clock, I haven't been waiting at all.

ART
I mean, there's not much to tell. I live in the town I grew up in. And I write books.

GWEN
Never married?

ART
No. I proposed once.

She grimaces.

GWEN
Sorry. Children?

ART
Yes actually.

Gwen is surprised.

GWEN
Really? You scoundrel you.

Art chuckles.

ART
Yes, that's me. Scoundrel.

GWEN
Blackguard.

ART
Rascal.

GWEN
Dastard.

ART
Excuse me? Oh, dastard. I like the sound of that actually.

Gwen puts her hand on his.

GWEN
Okay, enough literary posturing. Tell me the story.

ART
I'm not sure I can tell a story without literary posturing. I'd be thrown out of the Literary Fiction guild. We're very self-important.

GWEN
Just this once. Between us and Merle.

He sighs, leans back against the wall.

ART

I was living with someone. We weren't married. And she had a child. who was sharp and bright, and funny, and. And wise. Wiser than I was. And I adored her. So I unofficially adopted her.

GWEN

And her mother?

ART

Her mother and I split up after a couple of years. But. She's still my daughter. She lives on the West Coast now. But when she comes east, I get to see her.

Gwen smiles.

GWEN

See. Was that so hard?

ART

I'll let you know after the next guild meeting.

Gwen swivels again and relaxes against his shoulder.

GWEN

You're lucky.

ART

I know. You?

Gwen sighs.

GWEN

Not lucky. Not in that way.

ART

I'm sorry.

Gwen sits up again.

GWEN
I am too sometimes. But. Not often. It's like. Do you miss being able to leap tall buildings at a single bound? Well, no, it sounds nice but I never had it in my life so I don't miss it. I wonder sometimes what it would have been like. But even that, not often. Did you want kids?

Art laughs.

ART
Never occurred to me, honestly. Until it happened.

Gwen swivels and leans against his shoulder. He relaxes.

GWEN
I think,

She turns to him. The loss, the warm spot, the tiny pressure of her head against his shoulder, leaves him bereft.

GWEN
I think that is the way life should be, she continues. We shouldn't say life is meaningless without—whatever. Life is never meaningless, because it was never meant to be meaningful. That's us, that's our culture, our parents, our teachers telling us. But it's not true. We have no idea what life is supposed to be, because it's not supposed to be anything. Our species is a few hundred thousand years old, our language is far younger than that. How can we possibly think we have the words to explain life Maybe some species billions of years from now. But I doubt it.

ART

See. Pensive.

GWEN

No. Just a lot of time to read on the train. Okay. Maybe. So. No marriages. One child. How many books have you written?

ART

23.

GWEN

Don't get out much, do you?

ART

Visits from old friends are few and far between..

Gwen smiles and pats his face again. Then smacks him lightly.

GWEN

That's for using the O word.

She reaches into her bag and pulls out his book again.

GWEN

I thought I had read them all, but I haven't read anywhere near 23.

She turns to the inside flap.

GWEN

It lists six here.

ART

Only six of them are published.

GWEN

Six? Why? You're so good.

ART
Thank you. It's the way of the publishing world. Six published is good. Six is a lot.

Gwen looks at the book again.

GWEN
Wow. So you have seventeen books sitting in a drawer.

ART
Actually, they're in the Cloud, but yes, metaphorically speaking.

GWEN
Are they good?

Art thinks about his answer.

ART
They are—well-written.

GWEN
That sounds like a no.

ART
They aspire to sound like good books.

Gwen looks at him.

GWEN
I'd like to read them.

Art laughs, shakes his head.

I don't think...

He stops.

GWEN

What? she asks.

ART

I don't think I want you to remember me as the person who wrote them.

GWEN

Why is that important?

ART

I don't know. It wasn't an hour ago. An hour ago, I would have been happy for anyone to ask to read them. Though I still would have probably said no. I haven't read most of them in years. I can't vouch for them, I guess I am saying.

GWEN

I can see that. I get it. Still. 23 books in mphmfh years. That's an accomplishment.

Art laughs again, and she sees that this is his standard response to praise. And somehow that makes her sad, that he should think so little of something she admires so much.

ART

Of a sort, I suppose.

GWEN

It's impressive to me. I struggle with Christmas cards.

Now he shrugs. Back to the shrug, which is not as dismissive somehow as the laugh.

GWEN

So do I.

GWEN
Really? So. One thing we have in common.

ART
Meant for each other.

GWEN
Absolutely. We were meant to not write Christmas cards together until the end of time.

He shrugs again. But somehow it has changed, she thinks. Somehow it is Amused. Even Hopeful.

ART
It's something.

GWEN
Not exactly Heathcliff and Cathy.

His eyebrows climb half an inch on his face.

ART
It's the 21st century equivalent.

GWEN
Hmm. This does seem to be an unromantic century so far.

ART
There's still time.

GWEN
For the century, true.

ART
And for us.

GWEN
You think so?

ART
I'm not ready to rule it out.

GWEN
By us, do you mean you and me or do you mean us?

ART
I mean you and me. But I'm not ruling out us. We are having delicious coffee alone in a train station. That seems potentially romantic.

GWEN
Only to a romantic. Makes me wonder about those unpublished books.

He eyes her quizzically. Then shrugs. The new shrug, not the old one.

ART
Ask.

GWEN
Did they have happy endings?

He pauses, thinking through them. It takes a while—he can barely rememebr some of their titles.

I suppose you could say that. In a Dante-ish sort of way.

Gwen picks up his book, weighs it in her hand, and flips through the pages, placing her hand palm down on some as though she is trying to absorb by osmosis.

GWEN
Who is your favorite writer? she asks, not looking up from the book.

ART
Other than me.'

Now she looks up.

GWEN
Other than you.

ART
Actually we don't have to exclude me. There are many books I'd rather read than mine.

Gwen pauses, scrunching her face, as though the abstract thought process was slightly painful, then releasing at the conclusion.

GWEN
It's not the same thing, is it?

ART
What do you mean?

Gwen closes the book decisively, the better to argue her point.

GWEN
Books you'd rather read is different from favorite writer.

He doesn't respond.

GWEN
Art?

ART
Gwen?

Art and Gwen, they both think, for the first time. Art and Gwen again. There is a power in the mythos of those names. Their names conjoined are a charm.

GWEN
Are you okay? Not having a heart attack are you?

He shakes his head quickly.

ART
My heart is fine.

GWEN
Good. Because I only know the Heimlich maneuver. I don't know CPR.

ART
Noted.

GWEN
No. They are not the same.

ART
The Heimlich maneuver is not the same as CPR?

GWEN
No, A book you want to read most is not the same as favorite writer. Because a book you would rather read is affected by other factors, like how tired you are or what mood you're in. Favorite writer is the writer whose books mean the most to you.

Art laughs.

ART
Oh. Well. Then I am my favorite writer, but I'd rather read anyone else's books instead of mine.

GWEN
Why?

ART

I don't know about other writers, but by the time I finish one of mine I am sick of it. The only page of it I want to open is the one I sign my name to at a bookstore. Or train station.

GWEN

Your books, the published ones anyway, are warm and entertaining and thoughtful. I like them very much.

ART

Thank you. You are my target demographic.

GWEN

You mean women of a certain age?

ART

No. I mean you. I always write for you. Though I'm not sure if it's the you I remember or the you I imagine.

> *He watches her face carefully, tracking the evolution, in the eyes, which unfocus and focus twice, in the line in the jaw, which softens and firms in conjunction, and the arc of the lips. Especially the arc of the lips.*

GWEN

Really. Well. Good job.

> *Art sits back. They both feel like something has been said which needed to be said. But neither is quite cure what it was.*

Thank you.

> *Gwen lifts up the book, her exercise for the evening apparently. He notices, and knows he has lost a chance. He would not have the courage now. They have achieved something, and he fears he would disturb it, cancel it,*

whatever it is.

GWEN

No one's ever written anything for me before. Much less 23 books. I got a postcard once. But it was from my mother.

ART

What did it say?

GWEN

It didn't say anything. I suppose it was meant to be sort of proof of life.

Art lifts his head to the ceiling, thinking this through.

ART

I think that's what my books are. Proof of life.

Gwen nudges him with her shoulder.

GWEN

It's better than a postcard.

ART

In scale.

Gwen nudges him again.

GWEN

Now you're just being modest.

Art lowers his head, looks at her.

ART

They teach that at Author School too.

She turns, climbing up and kneeling on the bench, her white shoes barely revealed under her lavender dress.

GWEN
Hey Merle. Who's your favorite author?

Merle finishes a word and puts down the crossword.

MERLE
My favorite or the one I like to read most?

Gwen gives Art her fabled I-Told-You-So glance.

GWEN
Who's your favorite?

Merle goes back to his crossword, pencils in another line.

MERLE
Tolstoy.

GWEN
Really?

MERLE
In Russian. You have to read Tolstoy in Russian.

GWEN
You speak Russian?

MERLE
Ya uznal ot babushki. Ona by ne vyuchila angliyskiy.

GWEN
Ya ne vinyu yeye.

Merle nods.

MERLE
You speak Russian.

GWEN

Da.

Art turns and kneels on the bench.

ART

Hey Merle. Why Tolstoy?

MERLE

I only read one book a year, so it needs to last.

ART

There's Proust.

MERLE

I don't drink tea.

ART

Joyce.

MERLE

Juvenile sense of humor.

ART

And you find Tolstoy funny?

MERLE

In Russian, he's hilarious.

ART

So Tolstoy. Fine choice. War and Peace?

MERLE

That's good. But I prefer Anna Karenina.

GWEN

Me too.

Art glances at her.

                          GWEN

Has trains in it.

                           ART

True. Not a happy ending though.

                          GWEN

You'll just have to write your version.

>   *Pause. They drink. She looks at the clock, shakes her head.*

Why don't they fix that clock?

>   *Art looks at it. He gets up and walks toward it, stands under it for a moment.*

                           ART

Hey Merle?

                          MERLE

Yeah?

                           ART

Why don't they fix this clock?

                          MERLE

Cause everybody has a phone now. Nobody even looks at it nowadays.

>   *Art stares up at the clock.*

                           ART

Hey Merle? he says.

                          MERLE

Yeah?

                          ART
Have you got a ladder?

> *Gwen rises.*

                          GWEN
Art?

                          ART
Gwen?

> *She smiles. This look she knows, this intensity. She had never had a problem getting men's attention, though often getting men's attention was a problem in itself. But she remembered his face when he looked at her that way; as though he saw her completely, and through her completely. And in doing so, he also opened all of himself to you. When you were the object of that all-encompassing attention, it was unnerving, and exciting.*

                          GWEN
Don't hurt yourself.

                          ART
I'm just going to reset it. Maybe that will get it started. Where's the ladder, Merle?

                          MERLE
In the closet. But I'm not sure it's tall enough.

                          ART
We'll see.

> *Art goes to the closet and pulls out a ladder. Merle wanders over near the clock to observe.*

MERLE

I don't think the station insurance covers this. Actually, I don't think there is any station insurance.

Art places the ladder beneath the clock and starts to climb. Gwen rushes over to steady the ladder.

GWEN

You don't need to do this. It won't make a difference. The train will come when it comes.

He climbs down.

ART

It makes a difference. Not to the train, no. But it makes a difference.

She nods.

GWEN

I guess it does. Go for it.

He climbs the ladder.

ART

Hold it steady. I'm going to have to use the top step.

GWEN

Merle, would you help me, please?

Merle sidles up to the ladder and grabs one side, while she grabs the other.

ART

Got it? Art asks.

GWEN

Got it, Gwen says.

Arts reaches up, slips his hand behind the clock and finds the knob.

ART

What time is it now?

GWEN

Hold on.

She reaches down for her phone. The ladder sways. Art flattens himself against the wall and holds on.

GWEN

Three fourteen and a little, she announces.

He twists the knob clockwise, but the hands go backward. He twists it counterclockwise, and the hands spin forward, finally reaching three fourteen.

Art climbs carefully down the ladder and reaches the floor. They all stare up at the clock, hoping it will move. Nothing happens.

Then Merle walks to the wall and flips a switch. The second hand starts to turn.

MERLE

They turned it off in 2003. The clock always ran fast anyway.

Art turns to Gwen.

ART

They usually do.

She smiles. A train whistle sounds.

GWEN
That's my train. I hope.

ART
Do you?

GWEN
Less than I did before.

She rushes back to the bench, begins collecting her things. He follows.

ART
I'm glad I got to see you again.

Gwen glances at the clock.

GWEN
You are still an interesting man.

Then she frowns.

GWEN
Wait.

ART
What?

GWEN
The world is a sphere.

ART
So?

GWEN
The surface of a sphere is an arc.

ART
And?

                    GWEN
So trains travel in arcs.

> *Art lifts his head again, thinking, then glances at the clock.*

                    ART
I'll think I'll buy a ticket.

> *She stops collecting, looks at him.*

                    GWEN
Why?

> *Art turns to Merle, who has retreated to his cart..*

                    ART
Hey Merle?

                    MERLE
Yes?

                    ART
Do you have baseball caps for sale?

                    MERLE
Yeah, sure. Yankees. Red Sox. Mets. That's from 1986.

> *Art walks over to the cart.*

                    ART
86 Mets? That's perfect. How much?

> *Merle looks at the hat as if it is an old friend. Then he hands it to Art.*

                    MERLE
Take it. You're doing me a favor.

Art comes back and offers it to Gwen. She hesitates, then spins her hair into a ponytail and puts on the cap. Art steps back.

ART
Perfect. And there's one more reason.

Gwen adjusts the hat.

GWEN
Which is?

Art picks up her bags.

ART
I need to check out this arc thing. Could be a whole new old world.

GWEN
But you don't know where I'm going.

Art shrugs, this one with deep humor.

ART
Here to there. What else is there?

She pauses, then slowly nods.

GWEN
Let's find out.

She turns to Merle.

GWEN
Thank you, Merle. See you next trip.

Gwen and Art exit together under the clock and through the doors to the station platform just as the train is pulling in.

Merle sits back on his stool, takes up the crossword again.

MERLE
Must have been the mints.

Fade to Black

The End

No Surprise

Cast of Characters

CLERK Any age

PERSON Any age

Scene

Unknown.

Time

Eternity.

Act I Scene 1

Setting: A bare stage, except for a desk downstage center. Up left is a doorway. A bright light shines through it.

At Rise: A clerk is sitting at the desk, waiting, hands folded.

A Person enters. wanders around a bit, then approaches the desk.

CLERK
Welcome to Death.

PERSON
Where?

CLERK
Death.

Person nods.

PERSON
Where?

CLERK
Death. This is Death.

PERSON
So I'm dead?

CLERK
You people. Everything is all about you.

PERSON
Excuse me?

CLERK
That is one possibility.

PERSON
Excuse me?

CLERK
If you insist.

PERSON
Pardon?

CLERK
Well, that's a little more challenging.

PERSON
I don't think I understand.

CLERK
If you think, you don't understand.

PERSON
Excuse me?

CLERK
You're persistent. I'll give you that.

PERSON
Pardon?

CLERK
Anything is possible.

                        PERSON
So.

                        CLERK
Yep.

                        PERSON
And back when.

                        CLERK
Oh yeah.

                        PERSON
And then I.

                        CLERK
I would say so.

                        PERSON
So now.

                        CLERK
Almost there.

                        PERSON
This is.

                        CLERK
You can do it.

                        PERSON
Death.

                        CLERK
Hallelujah!

                        PERSON
Death?

CLERK
I knew you had it in you.

PERSON
Death?

CLERK
When you first entered, I thought to myself that is a person who has it in them.

PERSON
Death?

CLERK
Naturally.

PERSON
Death.

CLERK
Think nothing of it. Or anything else for that matter.

PERSON
I don't understand.

CLERK
That's because you have it in you.

PERSON
What is it?

CLERK
Obviously.

PERSON
So. This is death.

CLERK
This is death.

PERSON
And you are?

CLERK
Obviously.

PERSON
You don't have to be sarcastic.

CLERK
Oh. There is no sarcasm in Death.

PERSON
I see.

CLERK
That was sarcastic.

PERSON
I see.

CLERK
Just thought I'd mention that.

PERSON
I see.

CLERK
But sarcasm is not encouraged.

PERSON
Death isn't funny.

CLERK
Oh no. Comedy is encouraged. Death is very funny.

PERSON
So you say.

                    CLERK
So what can I do for you?

                    PERSON
I don't know. I just got here.

   The clerk laughs. For a long time.

                    CLERK
That's a good one. I have to remember that one. "I just got here".

                    PERSON
What can you do for me?

                    CLERK
What can't I do?

                    PERSON
I don't know. There seem to be a lot of rules.

                    CLERK
I wouldn't call them rules. More like improbabilities.

                    PERSON
I see. So what is probable?

                    CLERK
Likely.

                    PERSON
So what is likely?

                    CLERK
Probably.

                    PERSON
I don't think we're getting anywhere here.

CLERK
That anywhere is here is improbable.

PERSON
I'm not sure we're communicating.

CLERK
Who can say?

PERSON
So. Let me recap. I'm dead.

CLERK
Well done. Now that's what I call communication.

PERSON
I'm dead.

CLERK
Clear. Succinct. Almost true.

PERSON
Almost true?

CLERK
Very close. I would say really really in the vicinity. Except for the part that's wrong.

PERSON
Which part is that?

CLERK
The 'm.

PERSON
The 'm?

CLERK
Mmm.

PERSON
Mmm?

CLERK
Mmm.

PERSON
Hmmm

CLERK
No. Mmm.

PERSON
I think I've lost the thread.

CLERK
Then you don't need the needle.

PERSON
Needle?

CLERK
Or the camel. That's a myth.

PERSON
Are you saying I'm not dead?

CLERK
I was saying that. I'm not anymore.

PERSON
I'm not dead.

CLERK
I could say it again if it's helpful.

PERSON
Would you please?

CLERK
We are all about customer service. You. Are. Not. Dead.

PERSON
I'm not dead.

CLERK
Nope.

PERSON
But this is death?

CLERK
Yep.

PERSON
Death is.

CLERK
Obviously.

PERSON
Death is?

CLERK
You can do it!

PERSON
Death is a place?

CLERK
Can I get a ruling on that one?

The Clerk looks offstage and waits.

CLERK
Okay, we're going to give you that one. Ontologically it's a little shaky, but close enough.

PERSON
Death is a place.

CLERK
Think of it as "death is where you're at?" It helps if you lived during the 60s.

PERSON
I see.

CLERK
I'm glad.

PERSON
You said 'm.

CLERK
Oh let's not start that again.

PERSON
Finally we agree on something.

CLERK
And we agree on something final.

PERSON
So this is death.

CLERK
Yes.

PERSON
It's not what I expected.

CLERK
I expect not.

PERSON
I thought, maybe, angels. Choirs. Heavenly hosts.

CLERK
They're on break.

PERSON
Really?

CLERK
See, I told you sarcasm doesn't work here.

PERSON
I see what you mean.

CLERK
You can't see what I mean. I don't mean what can be seen.

PERSON
Well. It was a good life I guess.

CLERK
Really?

PERSON
On balance. Mostly. A lot.

CLERK
So you were a good person?

PERSON
On balance. Mostly. A lot.

CLERK
Good. I assume that's good.

PERSON
Don't you know? Isn't there some book somewhere that tells you, adds up the plusses and minuses and calculates the Goodness of my life.

CLERK
We try not to make those kinds of judgements.

PERSON
Oh.

CLERK
We leave that up to you.

PERSON
Oh. Oh?

CLERK
So?

PERSON
You're asking me if I was a good person?

CLERK
That was your criteria.

PERSON
What happens if I wasn't? Do I go to Hell?

CLERK
That's up to you.

PERSON
It's up to me?

The clerk shrugs.

CLERK
Think of me as a travel agent. I don't decide where you go, I just help you get there.

PERSON
So I will go somewhere?

CLERK
Again that's up to you.

PERSON
So how long do I have to stay here?

CLERK
We don't really like to deal in timeframes.

PERSON
Why?

CLERK
Because there aren't any.

PERSON
Why not?

CLERK
Because there isn't any time here.

PERSON
I'm here forever?

CLERK
You're here always. But not forever.

PERSON
Let's assume I understand that. So you're saying I have a choice?

CLERK
Do you want one?

PERSON
Yes.

CLERK
Are you sure?

PERSON
Yes.

CLERK
How did your last choice work out?

PERSON
Which choice?

CLERK
Life. How did that work out?

PERSON
I chose life?

CLERK
You were alive, correct?

PERSON
I was.

CLERK
Then you chose it.

PERSON
Why do you want to know?

CLERK
I'm curious.

PERSON
I'm just an average person.

CLERK
Then I'm really curious. I've never met one before.

PERSON
What? You must have met thousands.

CLERK
Uncounted multitudes. But never anyone average. Being average is incredibly rare.

PERSON
How long have you been here?

CLERK
I've been here since Always.

PERSON
That's confusing.

CLERK
Only if you think about it.

PERSON
Good point.

CLERK
I understand that you are experiencing this sequentially. But don't worry. You'll get over that.

PERSON
In time?

CLERK
Oh no.

Pause. Person is very confused. Clerk just smiles. Then get serious.

CLERK
So. How was life?

PERSON
You must know. You must have been alive sometime.

                    CLERK
No. Never made it to life.

                    PERSON
You were never alive?

                    CLERK
I don't think so.

                    PERSON
Then how did you get here?

                    CLERK
I applied online.

                    PERSON
No I mean. If you weren't born, why do you exist?

                    CLERK
One has nothing to do with the other.

                    PERSON
Really?

                    CLERK
As far as I know.

                    PERSON
Don't you know?

                    CLERK
You hear stories.

                    PERSON
Then you're not God?

                    CLERK
God I hope not. I would be really underpaid.

PERSON

Is there a God?

CLERK

You hear stories.

PERSON

So you have never met God?

CLERK

Not that I know of. I'm not sure I'd recognize it if I did.

PERSON

God is an it?

CLERK

In English. English doesn't have Eternal Pronouns. Yet.

PERSON

Are we speaking English?

CLERK

No, we're speaking American. I can speak English if you would like.

PERSON

No, that's okay.

CLERK

It would just muddy up the communication. We're already having a hard enough time.

PERSON

American is fine.

CLERK

So tell me about life?

PERSON
So. Life. What can I say. Its more interesting than death.

CLERK
Tell me about it

PERSON
Things happen one after another.

CLERK
Wow. Imagine that. What else?

PERSON
And once something happens, we don't know the next thing that's going to happen. Sometimes we think we know. But we can never be sure.

CLERK
That thinking thing seems like a real problem.

PERSON
It can be.

CLERK
Why do you do it?

PERSON
Once you start it's hard to stop.

CLERK
Ah.

PERSON
What else. What else. Well, we start out small and get bigger.

CLERK
As your brains expand from all the thinking.

PERSON
Not really. Actually we start losing brains cells as we age.

CLERK
Oh. Sorry.

PERSON
So. What else can I tell you? It's hard to talk about life with someone who hasn't lived.

CLERK
I can see that. Well, tell me this. Were you happy?

PERSON
Happy? Happy. Hmmm. Now that I think of it—

CLERK
Careful. Don't want your head to explode.

PERSON
Not likely. I guess. All in all. I wasn't happy. So much.

CLERK
I see.

PERSON
I mean. I did things. I loved people. I did things to people I loved.

CLERK
Love. I've heard of that. What is love?

PERSON
It's where you think of someone more than you think yourself.

CLERK
So love comes from thinking.

                    PERSON
No, come to think of it.

                    CLERK
So love comes from not thinking.

                    PERSON
No. You know. It's like. How to describe it. You know. You know. Like in the books.

                    CLERK
There are no books here.

                    PERSON
No books?

                    CLERK
No stories at all.

                    PERSON
No stories at all?

                    CLERK
None. Stories are a sequential effect. You need that one thing after another thing in a story.

                    PERSON
I would miss stories I think.

                    CLERK
Did they make you happy?

                    PERSON
No. But they made me forget I was unhappy.

                    CLERK
I'm sorry you weren't happy. Maybe next time.

PERSON
Next time. So there is a next time?

CLERK
Could be.

PERSON
So death isn't the end. It just keeps going. Forever. It never stops.

CLERK
As it will be in the beginning, was now, and ever used to be. Unless.

PERSON
Unless?

CLERK
You could have my job.

PERSON
Your job?

CLERK
I think you'd be good at it.

PERSON
Your job?

CLERK
You're a pleasant sort of person.

PERSON
Thank you.

CLERK
You're not very good at explaining things. But that is not really a criteria for the job.

PERSON
So I noticed.

CLERK
It's a good job really. You meet lots of interesting beings. It's a comfy chair. It swivels. Which is fun when things slow down. They'll say they'll work on the wifi.

PERSON
I don't think it's for me.

CLERK
There you go thinking again.

PERSON
Sorry.

CLERK
Where has that ever gotten you?

PERSON
Death?

CLERK
Exactly.

PERSON
I see what...I see.

CLERK
Stories. You like stories. We get some very good storytellers here. Aeschylus. Shakespeare. Rod Serling.

PERSON
Really?

CLERK
Yeah, he would have been great at this job. Had just the right voice.

PERSON
Oh yeah.

CLERK
I mean. Think about the life you just lived. Don't you want something new?

PERSON
Maybe. If it is such a good job, why would you give it up?

CLERK
Fair question.

PERSON
I think so.

CLERK
Honestly, I'm tired of never being surprised.

PERSON
Really?

CLERK
Yeah. I mean it's nice that I never forget to buy orange juice. But there is never anything new. Nothing changes. Everything always is.

PERSON
Not all surprises are pleasant, you know. For instance, death was a bit of a shock.

CLERK
I suppose. But. It is something I have never experienced. I only know everything. I mean, like stories. To not know how something ends. I can hardly imagine that.

PERSON
But you might not be happy. I wasn't.

CLERK
True. And I am happy here. Nothing happens.

PERSON
If I took the job, could I get out of it and go somewhere else?

CLERK
Sure. You just need someone to take your place.

PERSON
Ah. So that's it. You need me to say yes.

CLERK
Yes.

PERSON
I could stand a little happiness.

CLERK
More than a little. An eternity of happiness.

PERSON
Okay it's a deal.

They shake hands

PERSON
Hey wait. you knew I would say yes didn't you?

CLERK
I did. Here. Take a seat.

Person sits in the chair, undergoes the transition to eternal knowledge.

PERSON
So. Where would you like to go?

CLERK
I don't know. I don't know! How about that? I don't know something?

PERSON
Can I make a suggestion?

CLERK
Sure. That's your job now.

PERSON
Give life a try. If you pay attention, everything will surprise you.

CLERK
You know. It wouldn't surprise me.

PERSON
Okay then. See you next death.

Clerk waves and exits.

PERSON
Next!

Clerk enters, wanders around a bit, then approaches the desk.

PERSON
Welcome to Death.

Stephen Evans

Blackout

The End

Spooky Action at a Distance

A Play in Three Acts

Stephen Evans

"God does not play dice with the Universe."

Albert Einstein

"The dice of God are always loaded."

Ralph Waldo Emerson

STEPHEN EVANS

For my Angel.

Cast of Characters

HAROLD: A cosmologist, aging.

ANGEL: A dancer, ageless.

Scene

A hotel/casino in Las Vegas.

Time

Now.

STEPHEN EVANS

ACT I SCENE 1

Setting: A hotel room, not very plush. The room has one queen-size bed, a dresser, a chair, an old television, a mirror.

At Rise: The room is dark, except for a red blinking light seeping through the closed blinds, as though the world's biggest stop light had gone crazy outside.

The door opens. We hear casino bells—down the hall but VERY LOUD.

HAROLD stumbles into the room with a suitcase and a large artist's portfolio case. He is dressed in a tuxedo. The door closes behind him but stays slightly ajar.

Harold dumps everything into a jumble on the bed.

HAROLD
Let there be light.

He turns on a lamp, illuminating the room.

Harold removes a marker board and easel from the portfolio case. He sets up the easel and board, which has mathematical equations written on it:

Harold stands back and chuckles.

At the dresser, he empties his pockets, dumping many

silver dollars into a cardboard bucket that says Casino Voltaire. He places the suitcase on the dresser and removes a CD player (this could be a phone, or anything that can play music), a bottle of scotch, a bottle of pills, a gun, and a rope tied in a hangman's noose.

He swigs the scotch, and turns on the CD. The 'Of Science and Learning' section of Strauss' Thus Spake Zarathustra fills the room.

Harold shoves the bed under the ceiling fixture. He climbs up and ties the noose to the fixture. Then he climbs down, picks up the gun and the bottle of pills. He struggles to open the pills, finally succeeds, then pours them into his hand. He takes another swig but doesn't swallow, then climbs back on the bed, mouth full, gun in one hand and pills in the other.

He accidentally hits the noose with his head. It swings back and forth. He swings his head back and forth, trying to slip into it, unsuccessfully.

Then he hears a knock at the door.

> HAROLD
> *(through a mouth full of scotch)*

Hmm HuHmmm. (Go away).

There's another knock.

> HAROLD

Hmm HummmHmmm. (I'm busy).

There is another knock, very insistent.

HAROLD
Hmm HuHmmm HuhHuhHuh. (Go away, God dammit).

The door swings open.

The light in the hallway is blinding. Casino bells blast in.

ANGEL appears, framed in the doorway, in a very sexy angel costume with gossamer wings visible behind her, a little bent. Her halo is straight and gleaming.

Harold spits out the scotch.

Drops the pills.

Falls off the bed.

Accidentally squeezes the trigger.

The gun fires.

Angel drops to the floor.

Harold rises.

HAROLD
Oh my God. I killed an angel.

He looks up.

HAROLD
That's not good.

Harold puts the gun down, runs toward Angel, and slips on the pills on the floor.

He picks himself up, shakes his head, remembers what he was doing, runs toward Angel, slips again.

He picks himself up, shakes his head, remembers what he was doing, runs toward her, side steps that area of the floor, and kneels down in the hallway by her side.

He tries to wake her and can't, so he lifts her up, with some difficulty.

HAROLD
You'd think angels would be light.

He angles her this way and that, trying to get her wings through the door. Finally he succeeds by standing her up in the doorway, edging inside, and catching her as she falls through.

A bag or large purse sits next to the door. While balancing her, he picks it up with his foot and moves it inside. The door closes shut.

Harold takes Angel to the bed and puts her down. He checks her body for blood. Can't find any. He listens to her chest.

He climbs over her, starts CPR. As he is giving her mouth-to-mouth resuscitation, her eyes open.

ANGEL
HuHmmm HuhHuh. (This costs extra).

Harold sits up in shock.

ANGEL
This costs extra.

Harold realizes his hands are still on her chest and quickly pulls them off. In a crescendo of insight, they assert the obvious:

                    HAROLD
You're alive.

                    ANGEL
You shot me.

                    HAROLD
You're alive.

                    ANGEL
You shot me.

                    HAROLD
You're alive!

                    ANGEL
You shot me!

She shoves him off her, stands up on the bed, comes face to face with the noose, and screams.

Harold screams too.

Angel pummels Harold, chasing him off the bed, around the room.

                    HAROLD
I'm sorry! I'm sorry!

They retreat to neutral corners.

ANGEL	HAROLD
I don't have any money. You can check my purse. I don't have a purse. Check anything you want. Just don't hurt me.	I didn't mean to. It was an accident. I was up on the bed and the door opened and I fell and the gun went off.

Pause

ANGEL
What?

HAROLD
What?

ANGEL
Don't hurt me.

HAROLD
I never would.

She reassesses him.

ANGEL
Just stay where you are. Don't come near me.

HAROLD
It was an accident. I was up on the chair with the gun.

He picks up the gun.

and you came in and…you startled me.

ANGEL
Yeah, well, it was mutual.

He goes for the phone.

HAROLD
Do you want me to call a doctor?

ANGEL
No! I'm not hit. Just shook up. I must have fainted.

He hangs up.

HAROLD
The police will be here soon anyway. Someone will have heard the shot.

ANGEL
Not likely. We're next to the casino. Those slot machines have the decibel range of a jumbo jet.

He looks up at the ceiling.

HAROLD
What about cameras? I hear they watch everything in a casino.

ANGEL
Eye in the Sky. That's just in the casino, not in the rooms. Thank God.

She puts her hand to her head.

ANGEL
Maybe I'd better lie down.

She holds out her other hand to him, palm up.

HAROLD
Let me help you.

ANGEL
You want to make me feel better? Give me the gun.

He does.

ANGEL
Thanks.

He tries to help her to the bed. She holds him off.

ANGEL
Stop punctuating my equilibrium.

HAROLD
What?

ANGEL
I can do it.

She tries, sinks down and almost topples over. She holds out her hand to him, palm down this time.

ANGEL
Help me.

He rushes to her, helps her to the bed. She lays the gun down on the nightstand.

ANGEL
I must have hit my head when I fell.

HAROLD
I'll get some ice.

ANGEL
No, it's—

He throws open the door and rushes out. Casino bells blast in. The door closes automatically, shutting tight this time.

ANGEL
Okay.

She sees the strange equations on the board, chuckles.

There is a knock on the door.

ANGEL
Who is it?

HAROLD (OS)
It's me.
   (Pause)
I forgot my key.

> *(Pause)*

I forgot the ice bucket.

> *(Pause)*

This ice is really cold.

> *She sighs, lifts herself unsteadily off the bed, moves to the door, and opens it. He's holding the ice in his hands.*

HAROLD
Here.

> *He puts the ice in her hands.*

ANGEL
This ice is really cold.

HAROLD
Wait. I'll get an ice bucket.

ANGEL
No, it's—

> *He rushes out the door again. The door closes shut. She shrugs.*

ANGEL
Useless.

> *She dumps the ice in an ice bucket on the dresser. There's another knock.*

ANGEL
Who is it?

HAROLD (OS)
It's me again.

> *(Pause)*

I still don't have my key.

(Pause)
There aren't any ice buckets out here.
(Pause)
I'd really like to come in.

> *She shuffles back to the door and opens it.*

HAROLD
Thank you.

> *He spots the ice bucket on the dresser.*

HAROLD
I think we have the ice situation under control.

> *Angel wobbles a bit on her feet.*

HAROLD
Sorry. I shouldn't have. Let me.

> *He holds her arm, assists her to the bed again.*

HAROLD
How about a drink?

ANGEL
A drink would be good. No ice!

> *He pours two, sits on the bed and hands her a glass, keeping one for himself.*
>
> *She drinks hers down.*
>
> *Harold can't quite get his drink to his mouth because his hand is shaking. She watches this for a moment, then puts her hands around his to steady him. He takes a sip.*

HAROLD
Thanks.

She takes his glass and swallows the rest. She gives it back to him. He refills it.

ANGEL
By the way, happy—
        (*She pulls a card out of her costume*)
birthday.

HAROLD
Thanks. What?

He comes back. She takes the refilled glass.

ANGEL
I was paid to come and say that.

HAROLD
It's—

ANGEL
There was supposed to be dancing and nakedness too.

HAROLD
It's—

She drinks this one down too.

ANGEL
But since you shot me it no longer seems appropriate.

She hands him the glass.

HAROLD
It's not my birthday.

ANGEL
(Reading from the card)
Is this room two-six-zero?

HAROLD
If you say so.

He refills the glass again.

ANGEL
Are you...John?

HAROLD
Who?

She starts to take off her boots.

ANGEL
John. Are you John?

HAROLD
No, I'm Harold.

He holds out his hand, then ducks as her boot flies by him.

ANGEL
Stupid fucking switchboard. I hate it when this happens.

Harold drinks the scotch himself.

ANGEL
Unless your friends are playing a joke on you?

HAROLD
Not likely. I don't have any.

ANGEL
Stupid fucking switchboard.

Furious again, she takes off her other boot. Harold gets ready to dodge, but she holds on to it instead of throwing it.

ANGEL
They probably gave me the wrong fucking room number. Again.

HAROLD
So that's what Enochian sounds like.

She drops the boot down by the bed.

ANGEL
Fuck you, Harold.

HAROLD
I'm beginning to think you're not really an angel.

She makes a rude gesture. He holds out his hand to her.

HAROLD
Pleased to meet you.

She doesn't take his hand. But she relaxes a bit, propping herself up on the bed.

ANGEL
I could tell from the gunplay. I take it your usual target didn't show.

He's still holding out his hand.

HAROLD
Miss...

She still doesn't shake hands.

ANGEL
Call me Angel.

He pulls back his hand.

HAROLD
I can remember that.

ANGEL
I thought of it in a moment of perspiration.

HAROLD
You mean inspiration.

ANGEL
Not in my line of work.

She removes her halo, sets it on the nightstand next to the gun.

HAROLD
You're a dancer?

She considers him carefully.

ANGEL
Yes. Yes, I am.

HAROLD
What's your real name?

ANGEL
That's on a need-to-know basis, and you don't.

He looks hurt. She relents.

ANGEL
Ellie. My name is Ellie.

HAROLD
Ellie. Nice. Is that short for Ellen?

                    ANGEL
No.

   It's a puzzle.

                    HAROLD
Eleanor?

                    ANGEL
No.

   He has to figure out the answer.

                    HAROLD
Eloise?

   She realizes this could go on forever.

                    ANGEL
Eloa. It's short for Eloa.

   He sits on the uttermost edge of the bed.

                    HAROLD
Eloa. That's beautiful. I never heard that name before.

                    ANGEL
It's the name of an angel in some poem. My full name is Eloa Tiriel you don't need to know the rest.

                    HAROLD
Eloa Tiriel. No wonder you have a nickname.

                    ANGEL
My Father liked angels.

   Angel sits up, removes her left wing, which is attached with Velcro. Harold winces at the RIPPING sound.

ANGEL
Well, most of them.

She RIPS off the other one.

ANGEL
Here. Put these somewhere safe.

She hands the wings to Harold.

ANGEL
I never wanted to be an angel. When I grew up, I wanted to be a Dakini.

Harold is enthralled with the wings.

HAROLD
You wanted to be a bathing suit?

ANGEL
Dakini. Not Bikini.

HAROLD
Dakini. Sounds like something with Rum and Pineapple.

ANGEL
It's from Tibetan Buddhism. A Dakini is a Sky Dancer. She's like an angel only she drinks blood while dancing naked with a string of skulls around her neck.

Harold offers her the wings back.

HAROLD
You can go now.

ANGEL
I'm still a little dizzy.

HAROLD
Must be all that naked dancing.

He attaches the wings to the easel.

HAROLD
Here, I'll open a window.

Angel grabs for his arm as he goes to the window.

ANGEL
Don't! It's too bright out.

He shrugs her off.

HAROLD
It's after midnight.

He opens the blinds. A throbbing red light engulfs the room.

ANGEL
This is Vegas. You can get sunburn at 2 A.M.

He shuts the blinds.

ANGEL
Besides you can't open these windows.

She points to the liquor bottle and snaps her fingers.

ANGEL
They're afraid the losers will jump.

He stumbles half blind to the bottle on the dresser.

ANGEL
What was it? Craps? Blackjack?

He brings her the bottle.

HAROLD
What do you mean?

She takes a long drink. He watches, both alarmed and impressed.

ANGEL
How much did you lose?

HAROLD
I don't—

She points to the ice bucket and snaps her fingers.

ANGEL
You drop the kids college fund?

HAROLD
No.

ANGEL
Your retirement?

HAROLD
No.

He brings the ice to her.

ANGEL
Then what?

HAROLD
Nothing!

She tugs a pillowcase off a pillow.

ANGEL
You were trying to kill yourself.

She pours the ice in the pillowcase.

ANGEL
On the bed. With the gun. That you shot me with.

She twirls the pillowcase around over her head, twisting it into a ball at the end.

HAROLD
You're wrong.

She holds the icy ball to her head.

ANGEL
So I assumed you lost big.

He doesn't answer. She points to the noose.

ANGEL
Look. It was either that or you were practicing for Wild Bill's All Nude Rodeo down the street.

HAROLD
I said you're wrong.

ANGEL
Eight shows a day. Good money.

Harold again sinks down on the bed, facing away from her.

HAROLD
It's none of your business.

ANGEL
You made it my business when you shot me.

HAROLD
I didn't shoot you. I shot at you.

ANGEL
I'm so relieved. But why all this?

She swats at the noose.

ANGEL
Rope? Gun? Pills? How dead can you get?

He climbs up on the bed and starts taking down the noose.

HAROLD
I just wanted to be certain.

ANGEL
Certain? Of what?

HAROLD
Certain that I died.

ANGEL
I can see in your case it might be hard to tell.

Harold unties the noose and climbs down.

HAROLD
What do you mean?

ANGEL
Just that it's customary to live first.

HAROLD
I lived. Live. Am living.

ANGEL
You seem tenseless.

HAROLD
I am completely tense. Look. Okay, so I tried to kill myself. What are you going to do? Tell me everything's okay? Just talk it through and everything will be wonderful?

She considers, shrugs: her signature response to events.

ANGEL
Doesn't sound like me.

He puts the noose away.

HAROLD
You don't know anything about me.

ANGEL
When you carry firearms, you're not exactly a conversation magnet.

He goes to the door and opens it. Casino bells blast in.

HAROLD
Look. You seem like you're okay. I'm sorry if I scared you. If you need money, there's some in my wallet. Please take it and go.

She gets up and goes to the wallet. She looks in and fans out some bills.

ANGEL
Well, I guess you didn't lose everything.

Harold lets the door shut.

HAROLD
I've lost everything. And I'm not even a gambler.

She puts the bills back in the wallet.

ANGEL
Maybe you lost everything because you're not a gambler.

She looks at his credit cards.

ANGEL
If you're not here to gamble, why are you here?

> HAROLD

I'm here for a conference.

> ANGEL

Ah, the International Society of Suicides. I hear membership is declining.

She unfolds the clear plastic insert. No pictures.

> HAROLD

No, cosmology.

> ANGEL

The study of makeup.

> HAROLD

Not cosmetology. Cosmology.

> ANGEL

Big subject.

> HAROLD

There are more things in heaven and earth, Horatio, than are dreamt of in your philosophy.

She drops the wallet back on the dresser.

> ANGEL

Don't call me Horatio. Well, maybe the first part.

Harold goes to the door and opens it. Casino bells blast in.

> HAROLD

Look, I'm kind of busy here. I'd really like you to leave.

Angel goes to the board covered with equations.

> ANGEL

Are these your equations?

He lets the door swing shut. It closes tight this time too.

HAROLD
Please don't touch that. That's my suicide note.

She picks up the marker and puts little bells at the corner of the board.

HAROLD
Why did you do that?

ANGEL
It's Christmas.

HAROLD
Those equations are standard derivations of the theorem of Nonlocality. Also known as Bell's Theorem. Have you ever heard of Bell's Theorem?

ANGEL
No.

HAROLD
Would you like me to explain?

ANGEL
No.

Harold settles into his teaching voice and manner.

HAROLD
Bell's Theorem asserts—

ANGEL
No means no.

HAROLD
That there is some unknowable connection between elementary particles—

ANGEL
Just Say No.

HAROLD
Where when something happens to one of the particles—

ANGEL
There's no business like show business?

HAROLD
The other changes immediately, no matter how far apart they are.

Angel picks up her wings from the easel.

ANGEL
Did you ever see that movie where they say that every time a bell rings, an angel gets her wings?

HAROLD
It's called Entanglement. Though Einstein referred to it as spooky action at a distance.

ANGEL
I think the wingmaker must have been really pissed off when they invented slot machines.

Harold examines his equations and chuckles again.

HAROLD
It was a little inside joke for my colleagues. Suicide. Nonlocality. Bells. Seek not to know...

Angel puts the wings back.

HAROLD
Forget it.

ANGEL
SAAAD.

HAROLD
Not really.

ANGEL
That's what it spells. Spooky Action At A Distance.

She writes in the air.

ANGEL
S-A-A-A-D. SAAAD.

HAROLD
Do you always think in acronyms?

ANGEL
Just something my mind does automatically.
She writes in the air again.
JSMMDA.

HAROLD
Now that's SAAAD.

ANGEL
Sometimes I think entirely in acronyms. SITEIA. Saves time.

HAROLD
ST. I get the picture.

ANGEL
Spooky action at a distance. That describes every boyfriend I ever had.

He refuses to be distracted.

HAROLD
Look. I'm trying to do something important here.

He goes to the door and opens it. Casino bells blast in.

                    HAROLD
Please leave.

                    ANGEL
So I imagine you've thought this through.

He slams the door shut in frustration.

                    HAROLD
Of course I've thought it through.

She goes to the dresser, plays with the coins.

                    ANGEL
Thought it through completely, like the intelligent man you are. If you don't mind my using that term.

                    HAROLD
Yes. Completely. Completely through. Why?

She notices the CD player, is a little surprised, fingers the buttons.

                    ANGEL
I was just wondering what you wish to come back as?

                    HAROLD
What do you mean?

                    ANGEL
You know. Reincarnation.

                    HAROLD
There's no such thing as reincarnation.

She takes out the CD.

                    ANGEL
Are you sure?

HAROLD
There's no convincing scientific evidence supporting it.

She doesn't recognize it, puts it back.

ANGEL
Are you 'certain'?

ANGEL	Harold
I think you're getting your epistemology confused with your ontology. I mean positivism is empirically useful, but it is by definition as self-limiting as, say, phenomenology.	Of course I'm not certain. The point is. The point is. Certainty is, in physics, in anything. The point is, which they don't see, is that I'm here because, because, because I don't know why I'm here.

Pause

ANGEL	Harold
What?	What?

Pause

ANGEL	Harold
It is the height of arrogance to say that only what I can see and measure can be real, especially for creatures who haven't been around that long on the universal scale.	We are an unintended complexity, an undesired byproduct floating over an essential reality that not only doesn't care, but is fundamentally

unaware, that we even exist.

Pause

ANGEL
What?

HAROLD
What?

He sighs. Now he goes for the scotch.

HAROLD
You can't have reincarnation without something to reincarnate. I see no evidence that people have souls. To me, the evidence seems quite to the contrary.

ANGEL
Oh I can prove you have a soul.

She begins to stretch.

HAROLD
You can prove it? Logically?

More stretching.

ANGEL
A completely logical proof.

HAROLD
That I would like to hear.

ANGEL
Okay.

She jumps onto the bed.

ANGEL
Fuck me.

Harold turns away.

HAROLD
I…uh…uh…no. Thank you.

Angel sits up in Lotus position.

ANGEL
See? There you go. You have a soul.

HAROLD
Because I wouldn't…

ANGEL
No. Because you have free will.

He glances back.

HAROLD
Oh…I…uh…well?

She writhes sensuously on the bed.

ANGEL
And you can't have free will without a soul.

His curiosity overcomes his embarrassment.

HAROLD
How do you figure?

ANGEL
Simple. Free will can't exist in a strictly material process.

Angel again moves into Lotus position.

ANGEL
Look, logically, any physical process has to be either random or non-random, right?

HAROLD
One or the other, I guess. Sure.

She evolves into another yoga position, more erotic.

ANGEL
If your decision process is random, then it's not free will because it's not will at all. There's no intent. It's random.

HAROLD
Wait.

She twists into a third yoga position.

ANGEL
Now if your decision process is not random.

Then leaps into a cartwheel.

ANGEL
Then each decision point is equivalent to a determinative physical state, and the decision process is simply a computation of these various physical states using some biochemically inspired algorithm.

Into a handstand.

ANGEL
No matter how complex the algorithm, it's still not free will because each state is physically pre-determined.

HAROLD
Wow.

She walks up to him on her hands.

ANGEL
Free will is really free. And to be really free, it must have a non-physical source.

She flips to an upright position.

ANGEL
Hence the soul.

She falls backward onto the bed.

ANGEL
Hence, reincarnation. Hence—

She transforms again into the Lotus position.

ANGEL
What do you wish to come back as?

Harold backs away.

HAROLD
You know, I bet I do have free will. My decision-making process could never have evolved naturally. I'd be extinct by now.

Moving her hands like an Indian dancer.

ANGEL
Stop avoiding the issue.

Harold brightens.

HAROLD
I know. I'll come back as God.

ANGEL
Bad choice.

HAROLD
Why?

ANGEL
You'd have only yourself to blame.

                    HAROLD
True.

                    HAROLD
You tell me. What do you see me coming back as?

> *She considers him closely for a moment, intensely enough to make Harold self-conscious.*

                    ANGEL
A train whistle.

                    HAROLD
Why?

                    ANGEL
Because no matter where you are you're always leaving.

> *Harold then considers her. She is completely comfortable, which makes him uncomfortable.*

                    HAROLD
Do you know what I see you as? A cloud.

> *She is charmed by his answer.*

                    ANGEL
Really? That's sweet!

                    HAROLD
Because no matter where you are, you're always raining on something!

                    ANGEL
Oh.

                    HAROLD
I'm trying to commit suicide here and I want to feel good about it.

ANGEL
Well, I'm sorry.

She is. He relents.

HAROLD
It's not your fault. You're just optimistic.

ANGEL
I'm just as depressed as you are.

HAROLD
You are not.

ANGEL
I am too.

HAROLD
You're practically cheerful. You come in here "la la la, I'm an angel". You virtually floated in here.

ANGEL
I virtually floated in here because I fainted after you shot me.

HAROLD
That is just...just...Just. But the point is I'm suicidal and you're leaving.

He goes to the door and opens it.

Casino bells blast in.

ANGEL
I'm not leaving.

HAROLD
Yes you are.

ANGEL
What are you going to do? Shoot me again?

He lets the door close.

HAROLD
No. No. Look. Please. This is very private. I can't kill myself with an audience.

ANGEL
Why?

HAROLD
It would be rude.

ANGEL
Rude?

HAROLD
Rude. It would be rude.

Angel moves to the gun.

ANGEL
Okay. Okay. I'll leave.

She picks up the gun.

HAROLD
Thank you.

She moves to the door, squeezes between the door and Harold.

ANGEL
With you.

They are very close. This time Harold doesn't back off. But her proximity is very disconcerting.

HAROLD
Look. I appreciate what you're trying to do. But it won't work. There's nothing you can do to stop me.

ANGEL
I'm not trying to stop you.

HAROLD
You're a very sweet person to try and—what?

ANGEL
I'm not trying to stop you.

HAROLD
You're not?

She points the gun at her head.

ANGEL
I'll leave with you.

Harold is puzzled at first, then understands—she's proposing a double suicide.

HAROLD
No.

ANGEL
Yes.

HAROLD
You mean?

ANGEL
Yes.

HAROLD
No!

ANGEL
Yes!

She stops him from speaking by putting the gun to his lips.

ANGEL
Don't argue. It's rude.

Now he moves away, trying to get his mind around the concept.

HAROLD
Why?

Angel's eyes flash with anger.

ANGEL
What? You think I can give you a two-minute monologue that will explain my life to you, that will explain my pain to you, the losses I have suffered from which I will never recover, from which no one ever recovers?

HAROLD
I'm sorry.

ANGEL
You can't derive this from the sum of my histories.

Harold is taken aback by the phrase.

HAROLD
That's quantum physics.

ANGEL
What?

HAROLD
Sum of my histories. That's what you do to a particle. To calculate the probability of an event, you sum up the possible histories of the—

She holds up the gun.

ANGEL
Make up your mind. Do you want to talk or do you want to...not talk.

HAROLD
What? No. You are free to do what you want on your own, but if you want to do this with me, I need to know why.

She looks in the mirror.

ANGEL
How's this: the soul is like a jukebox. There are lots of songs inside. If you don't like the current song, push the button and make your next selection.

HAROLD
Won't this give you bad Karma or something?

She laughs.

ANGEL
Oh yeah, I'm just really racking up the good Karma in this life.

HAROLD
But you're not like me. You're smart. You're beautiful.

ANGEL
You're sweet, Harold. Naïve but sweet. In this life, I'll always be...Horatio.

HAROLD
You're wrong.

ANGEL
This is my chance.

HAROLD
Chance for what?

She pulls his arm around her. The hand with the gun is at her breast.

ANGEL
To not die alone.

He nods. This he understands.

HAROLD
Entanglement.

ANGEL
Exactly.

HAROLD
Okay.

Angel claps her hands. The decision made, she is all business.

ANGEL
So. How do we do it?

HAROLD
Do it?

ANGEL
Should we stab each other?

Harold winces.

HAROLD
Won't that hurt?

ANGEL
Think how effective it will be.

HAROLD
I don't have any knives.

ANGEL
Bayonets? Swords? Scissors?

HAROLD
Sorry.

ANGEL
I thought all men carried something sharp.

HAROLD
I used to carry a fountain pen. But it jammed.

ANGEL
A common problem in men your age.

She takes the gun.

ANGEL
Well then, you could shoot me—you have some experience at that—then shoot yourself.

HAROLD
That won't work.

ANGEL
Why not?

Harold takes the gun and removes the clip. It's empty.

HAROLD
There was only one bullet in the gun.

ANGEL
Who buys only one bullet?

She examines the clip.

HAROLD
I didn't want anyone else to get hurt by accident.

She gives it back.

ANGEL
That was very polite of you, considering you'd be dead.

He drops the empty clip and gun on the dresser.

HAROLD
Anyway, I was sort of hoping to be asleep when I killed myself.

ANGEL
Pills! That will work.

He glances down.

HAROLD
They were in my hand. Now they're all over the floor.

She goes to her purse, reaches in, pulls out a bottle of pills.

ANGEL
Here. We can use these.

HAROLD
Oh. What are they?

ANGEL
Trust me. They'll do the job.

She opens the childproof cap.

ANGEL
The guy who sold them to me promised. And he's killed enough people to know.

HAROLD
What are you doing with them?

She gives him a look: isn't it obvious?

HAROLD
Oh. I see. But there are two of us now.

ANGEL
Enough to kill a chorus line, that's what he said. Trust me on this.

Harold nods. They head for opposite sides of the bed.

HAROLD
You say "trust me" a lot.

ANGEL
If you can't trust an angel, who can you trust?

He can't argue with that.

HAROLD
Well, let's do it.

She starts to take off her costume.

HAROLD
What are you doing?

She stops.

ANGEL
I'm getting ready to do it.

HAROLD
Do what exactly?

ANGEL
I'm getting undressed.

HAROLD
I see that. Why?

ANGEL
It's customary.

HAROLD
What is?

ANGEL
When you commit suicide, you have to be naked.

She crawls over the bed to his side.

ANGEL
It's the rule.

HAROLD
No one ever told me that.

She helps him off with his jacket.

ANGEL
Don't you remember that movie, A Star is Born?

She unhooks his cummerbund.

ANGEL
At the end, when James Mason walks down to the ocean, he drops his robe.

HAROLD
You mean?

ANGEL
Buck.

She takes off his bow tie.

HAROLD
But he was English?

ANGEL
That's why he followed the rule.

HAROLD
Why, though?

She slides down his suspenders.

> ANGEL
> I don't know.

She unbuttons his shirt.

> ANGEL
> Maybe that way, the people who find you can at least think you had some fun first.

> HAROLD
> Oh. I always thought you dressed up for suicide.

She undoes the cufflinks.

> ANGEL
> Oh no. Black tie is definitely wrong. Nudity is proper for double suicide.

She pulls off his shirt.

> HAROLD
> That has no basis in rational thought.

> ANGEL
> De gustibus non disputandem est.

> HAROLD
> Excuse me?

> ANGEL
> Don't they teach Latin anymore? I said there is no disputing taste.

She rests her hands lightly on his chest.

> ANGEL
> Unless of course you're a televangelist.

                    HAROLD
Wait. Let me turn out the light.

> *Angel shrugs and gets in bed.*

                    ANGEL
Suit yourself.

> *He turns out the light. The pulsing red neon glare filters through the curtains, alternately illuminating the room dimly and leaving it dark.*

                    HAROLD
I have the pills. Here are yours.

> *He blindly tries to find her hand, and finds other things instead.*

                    HAROLD
Oh, sorry! I didn't mean…I mean…

                    ANGEL
It's okay.

                    HAROLD
I'm a little nervous.

                    ANGEL
Me too.

                    HAROLD
It's my first suicide.

                    ANGEL
Mine too.

> *Harold takes charge.*

                    HAROLD
Okay. We swallow on three.

ANGEL
Don't worry. I'm a professional.

HAROLD
One.

ANGEL
One.

HAROLD
Two.

ANGEL
Two.

HAROLD
Three.

ANGEL
Three.

Neither moves.

HAROLD
Did you?

ANGEL
No.

HAROLD
Are you afraid?

ANGEL
Yes.

HAROLD
Me too.

He sighs. Then she sighs.

HAROLD
You know what I'm afraid of most? That it won't be the end. That my mind will just go on and on and on with nothing to stop it, forever.

ANGEL
Like Televangelists.

HAROLD
Exactly.

Angel moves closer to him.

ANGEL
In the books, they say admit what you fear.

HAROLD
I just did.

ANGEL
I mean embrace it.

Angel moves next to him. She puts her hand to his cheek, turns his head toward her.

ANGEL
I'll put them in your mouth and you put them in mine.

HAROLD
That's assisted suicide.

ANGEL
So they can put us in jail afterwards.

HAROLD
Oh right. Okay, it's a deal.

ANGEL
Here, take a drink first.

She gives him a drink from the bottle of scotch.

ANGEL
Ready? On three. One. Two. Three.

They swallow.

HAROLD
Did you?

ANGEL
Yes.

HAROLD
Me too.

Angel sits on the bed, back against the headboard. Harold joins her. There is a long pause.

HAROLD
Why couldn't this have happened last night?

ANGEL
What?

HAROLD
Nothing.

She settles in next to him.

ANGEL
You have a nice mouth.

HAROLD
So do you. You have nice eyes.

ANGEL
You can't see my eyes.

HAROLD
I know. I just...you sound like you have nice eyes.

ANGEL
Would you hold me, Harold?

HAROLD
Oh God yes.

ANGEL
Are you feeling sleepy yet?

HAROLD
I don't feel anything. Honest.

ANGEL
I'm not sleepy yet either.

She snuggles into him.

ANGEL
Closer.

HAROLD
Yes, it's closer.

ANGEL
Hold me closer.

He does.

HAROLD
Like that?

ANGEL
Just.

HAROLD
So.

Harold laughs nervously.

                    HAROLD
There's something I've always wanted to know. How many angels can dance on the head of a pin?

She rolls on top of him.

                    ANGEL
Depends on the size of the pin.

She kisses him.

Blackout

End Act I

STEPHEN EVANS

Act II Scene 1

Setting: The Twilight Zone

At Rise: A door floats in empty space against a backdrop of stars. Harold is standing in front of the door.

The door swings open. Angel is framed in a blinding blinking red light.

HAROLD
Who are you?

ANGEL
I'm the Angel of Death.

Harold breaks out in laughter.

ANGEL
What?

Blackout

STEPHEN EVANS

Act II Scene 2

Setting: The Twilight Zone

At Rise: A door floats in empty space against a backdrop of stars.

Harold speaks using a microphone from the back of the theater, as in the musical A Chorus Line.

HAROLD
Number...260?

A reddish spotlight flares. Angel reluctantly walks through the door into the spotlight. She peers beyond the stage.

ANGEL
That's me.

HAROLD
What's your name?

ANGEL
Angel.

HAROLD
I didn't ask what part you were auditioning for. I asked your name.

ANGEL
Angel. That is my name. My stage name.

She starts looking around for something.

HAROLD
I see. Okay, what part are you auditioning for?

ANGEL
Angel.

HAROLD
How convenient.

ANGEL
I thought of it—

HAROLD
I know. What number are you going to do?

A CD player appears in another spot.

ANGEL
I'm not sure I have the right music.

HAROLD
Look Miss...Angel, we don't have forever. Well, actually, we do, but...

ANGEL
I understand. Okay.

She starts the CD player, then runs into place center stage. The music of Thus Spake Zarathustra booms out, the same segment Harold was playing earlier.

Angel performs her graceful and erotic Angel Dancer.

Before she's finished, Harold interrupts her.

HAROLD
Thank you.

She switches off the music.

HAROLD
We'll call you.

Angel nods. She knows what that means. She's almost out the door when:

HAROLD
Honestly, I'm not sure you're angel material.

ANGEL
But that's all I want to be.

HAROLD
Look, I realize that these are very subjective judgments, but I am the Director.

She heads downstage and speaks into the darkness.

ANGEL
You may be the Director but you aren't God.

HAROLD
Well...okay, look, I'm a merciful guy. Tell me something: what is it that you want to do most?

Angel starts to speak. He cuts her off.

HAROLD
Don't say be an angel. Don't tell me what you want to be. What do you want to do?

ANGEL
I want to...discover a cure for cancer.

HAROLD
I see. Anything else?

ANGEL
I want to...end world hunger.

                    HAROLD
              (bored)
I see. Anything else?

   She's desperate.

                    ANGEL
I want to dance!

                    HAROLD
I see.

                    ANGEL
It's what I do.

                    HAROLD
I see.

                    ANGEL
It's what I do!

                    HAROLD
I see.

                    ANGEL
Anything else?

                    HAROLD
              (Muttering to himself)
I have enough damned angels as it is.

                    ANGEL
I see.

   Harold sighs, LOUDLY, a Dolby rumble that shakes the theater.

                    HAROLD
Tell the costumer to redo those wings. I don't want them drooping on stage. Got it?

                    ANGEL
Yes, sir. Thank you, sir.

                    HAROLD
Now get out of here.

                    ANGEL
You won't regret it.

                    HAROLD
I never do.

   Blackout

STEPHEN EVANS

Act II Scene 3

Setting: The Twilight Zone

At Rise: A door floats in empty space against a backdrop of stars. Harold is standing in front of the door.

The door swings open. Angel is framed in a blinding blinking red light.

HAROLD
Who are you?

Harold breaks out in laughter.

ANGEL
What?

Blackout

STEPHEN EVANS

Act II Scene 4

Setting: The Twilight Zone

At Rise: A door floats in empty space against a backdrop of stars. Harold and Angel are standing in front of the door.

Harold looks around.

HAROLD
Where am I?

ANGEL
You're dying.

He points at her, nervous as Scrooge on Christmas eve.

HAROLD
Who are you?

ANGEL
I'm the angel of near-death.

Harold drops the nervous act and corrects her.

HAROLD
Don't you mean the angel of death?

ANGEL
I'm working my way up.

Back to Scrooge, quaking.

HAROLD
Why are you here?

ANGEL
It's a job.

HAROLD
No. I mean. Why Are You Here?

Angel gestures like a model on a game show.

ANGEL
(bored)
I'm here to show you what life would be like if you had never lived.

Harold is delighted. He was in the wrong movie.

HAROLD
Oh. I got it. Like the movie. Go ahead.

He looks around expectantly, which makes her look around too. He gestures: Well?

ANGEL
This is it.

HAROLD
What do you mean this is it? I don't see anything.

ANGEL
Of course you don't. You're dead.

He looks around again.

HAROLD
But this is boring.

ANGEL
You're telling me. I can't wait to get promoted.

HAROLD
No. I mean not living is boring. Really boring.

ANGEL
Yeah. Boy, did you make a mistake.

HAROLD
It's not funny.

She holds up a deck of cards.

ANGEL
I brought a deck of cards.

She starts shuffling.

HAROLD
Wait! This isn't right. You're supposed to show me all the terrible things that would have happened if I never lived.

ANGEL
Oh yeah. I always forget that part.

She peers off toward the audience.

ANGEL
Nope. Everything is fine.

HAROLD
What do you mean everything is fine? Check again.

ANGEL
Okay.

She peers off toward the audience again. She starts to laugh.

ANGEL
Oh yeah, they're having fun. Party time!!!

HAROLD
What?

ANGEL
Your sister got your room. She loved that.

HAROLD
Wait, what about my brother? I saved him from drowning.

ANGEL
Well, yes, but you were the one who wanted to go swimming in the first place. He went to a baseball game instead. Met a cheerleader.

HAROLD
So it didn't matter?

ANGEL
Well, I mean come on. You are just a bit of unintended complexity, you know that.

She starts to deal the cards.

Blackout

Act II Scene 5

Setting: The Twilight Zone

At Rise: A door floats in empty space against a backdrop of stars. Harold is standing in front of the door.

Playwright's Note: the letters in the following lines are each pronounced individually, as in an acronym (or Initialism, to be precise)/

HAROLD

W A Y.

ANGEL

I A T A O D.

HAROLD

D B N P, T S H C T

M A D, F T A N S;

F T W T T T D O,

D N, P D, N Y C T K M.

F R A S, W B T P B,

M P; T F T M M M F,

A S O B M W T D G,

R O T B, A S D.

Stephen Evans

T A S T F, C, K, A D M,

A D W P, W, A S D;

A P O C C M U S A W

A B T T S; W S T T?

O S S P, W W E,

A D S B N M; D, T S D.

                     Angel
O K.

   BLACKOUT

Act II Scene 6

Setting: The Twilight Zone

At Rise: A door floats in empty space against a backdrop of stars. The door has shrunk to the size of a podium and Harold stands behind it. There is a huge book on the podium, thousands and thousands of pages long. To the side, a blank white board on an easel, also elongated out of shape.

HAROLD
It's a bit dark in here.

ANGEL (VO)
Let there be light.

Harold is hit by a brilliant blue spotlight.

HAROLD
Someone's been reading ahead.

Harold clears his throat, drinks some water.

HAROLD
Welcome to Divinity School.

There's a general voiceover muttering from the invisible 'audience'.

HAROLD
I know. Someone of you are wondering 'Why?'

The muttering gets louder.

> HAROLD
>
> I'm all powerful. I'm omniscient. Why do I have to attend a conference on how to be a god?"

Harold holds out his hands, calming.

> HAROLD
>
> Every god thinks he's ready to direct a universe. But what we will present to you at this conference will save you eons of bad reviews. So let's get started.

He claps his hands. Thunder sounds.

> HAROLD
>
> The first thing I want to go over is the curriculum vitae. If you'll turn your workbooks to page six times ten to the minus 15.

He turns the pages in the enormous book, back and back and back to the first page.

> HAROLD
>
> In the beginning will be the word. Please do not repeat the word to others. If you do, we have to pick another word and it means reprinting a lot of stationery.

He turns a page, then puts on reading glasses.

> HAROLD
>
> Day One: Divide light from darkness. Call the light Day and the dark Night. Apply quality control techniques and see that it is good.

Another page.

HAROLD
Day Two: Divide the waters from the waters. Make the Earth and seas. Invest in real estate in Malibu. See that it is Oceanfront.

Another page.

HAROLD
Day Three: Let the earth bring forth grass. Talk about lawn care.

Another page.

HAROLD
Day Four: Set lights in the firmament of heaven. Emphasize the importance of proper lighting.

Another page.

HAROLD
Day Five: Bring forth living creatures. Remind me to mention snakes.

Another page.

HAROLD
Day Six: Create male and female. Be fruitful and multiply. By the way, this is not a section about mathematics.

And finally.

HAROLD
Day Seven: Take a break.

He takes off his reading glasses.

> HAROLD

Let's please try and keep the break to no more than 13.8 billion years.

He closes the book with an enormous crash that resounds throughout the known universe.

> HAROLD

But before we move on to Day One, I want to throw out a question for you: Why? Why do you want to direct a universe?

Some of the answers I've heard before are:

a) I'm bored.

b) It's lonely at the top.

c) All the other gods have one.

What do you think about those answers?

Angel in VO makes a rude noise.

> HAROLD

Exactly. None of those answers are very satisfying, are they? So you have two choices. You can spend ages in analysis trying to understand your inner Godot. Or you can think in these terms: what do you want your universe to do?

He begins to pace across the stage.

> HAROLD

Most universes do something; they are active, not static. Static universes are really only good for Christmas presents. They look great in one of those little crystal balls where you shake them up and watch the galaxies float around.

He stops in front of the white board and picks up a

marker.

HAROLD
But for the long run, and, trust me, eternity is a long run, you need an active universe. By definition, an active universe has a Purpose.

He writes PURPOSE on the white board.

HAROLD
So the first question you have to answer as a director is what is the purpose of the universe.

He goes back to the podium, consults his notes.

HAROLD
Here's a hint. Pick an action verb. Something simple. I know, you all think you're ready for parallel universes of infinite number. But frankly, that just takes too long to grade. So, something simple. To Worship. To Love. To...

ANGEL (VO)
Dance?

He's pleased.

HAROLD
Dance!

He writes DANCE on the board.

HAROLD
Okay, that's good. So. Dancing is your purpose. How would you set up the universe?

No answer.

HAROLD
What do you need?

ANGEL (VO)
Space.

HAROLD
Exactly. If you want dancing, you need.

He writes SPACE on the board.

HAROLD
And lots of it. You don't want your dancers cramped into a tiny stage. And not just space, you need mostly...

ANGEL (VO)
Empty space?

HAROLD
Exactly.

He writes EMPTY before space on the board.

HAROLD
You don't want your dancers tripping over things either. One misplaced black hole can do a lot of damage, trust me.

He points to the cluttered event horizon behind him.

HAROLD
So you want your space uncluttered for the most part. Okay, you have empty space. What else do you need? Anyone? Any duality? Any trinity?

ANGEL (VO)
Time.

HAROLD
Exactly. To dance, you need motion. And for motion you need.

He writes TIME on the board after space.

          HAROLD
Time is one of the hardest concepts for eternal beings to comprehend.

He draws a bell on its side.

          HAROLD
Look at this illustration. This is what time looks like to us: motion through multiple dimensions. Nothing is lost. Time is growth.

He draws perpendicular lines through the bell.

          HAROLD
Now observe.

He points.

          HAROLD
These lines are what motion looks like from within space-time. You can see that there is a sense of one thing replacing another at each point on the cone. Got it? Well make some time and work on it.

Okay, we have space. We have time. What else do we need?

          ANGEL (VO)
Dancers.

          HAROLD
Makes sense, right? Can't have dancing without—.

He writes DANCERS on the board.

          HAROLD
So what kind of dancers do we want?

> ANGEL (VO)

Beautiful. Flowing. Light.

> HAROLD

Beautiful flowing light.

He writes LIGHT on the board.

> HAROLD

We want to fill our universe with—

> ANGEL (VO)

Beautiful flowing light, dancing, spinning, waving, filling the fabric of the empty universe with rapturous, ecstatic motion.

> HAROLD

There's your mission statement.

He puts down the marker.

> HAROLD

Now as a director, eventually you are going to want to just sit back and watch, not take an active eon to eon part in the dance, but just enjoy it as it unfolds before you. Once you get to this point, you will need to add...

> ANGEL (VO)

Dance captains.

> HAROLD

Exactly. Dance captains. These dance captains, also known as,

He writes ANGELS on the board.

> HAROLD

Will keep the action moving according to your divine orders.

So. That's our project. Our universe. Dance-Empty-Space-Time-Light-Angels. So how do we start?

There is muttering but no answer.

HAROLD
All you have to do is ring a bell. Every time a bell rings, a universe is born. This is known as Bell's Theorem.

He laughs.

HAROLD
Now of course, it's not quite that simple, as you might expect. You have to ring the bell with just the right tonality to produce the appropriate cosmological constants. Yes, question?

A red spotlight hits Angel, who is sitting in the audience.

ANGEL
As a director, do you show or tell? In other words, do you get up on stage and show the dancers what to do, or do you stand outside the dance and direct.

Harold sits on the edge of the stage and talks to her.

HAROLD
Excellent question. My preference is to stand outside. Your dancers learn more. Plus you keep your perspective.

Angel raises her hand. He calls on her.

ANGEL
So how do you teach?

HAROLD
For 99.9999999% of creation, you won't need to. But for the few, the special, the conscious, you need to work a little harder.

ANGEL
How do you do that?

HAROLD
Several ways. You can issue—

He goes back to the podium, puts his glasses back on.

HAROLD
Commandments.

He takes off his glasses.

HAROLD
Commandments can be very effective. But be careful how many you issue. Ten is too many. Nobody can remember ten commandments. I say, pick your top three. Personally, I prefer: Love your God, Dance with Beauty, and Smile at the Audience. Short, clear, and to the point.

He steps out from behind the podium.

HAROLD
Which reminds me. I know some of you think that writing your commandments in stone is the way to go. But, trust me, stone is just too bulky. I have found more discarded commandments at yard sales than I'd care to mention.

Angel is taking careful notes.

ANGEL
What if commandments don't work?

HAROLD
Well, then you can try writing a sacred text. If you don't have time to write it yourself, you can use a ghost writer.

He sits at the edge of the stage again.

HAROLD
But here's a tip: If the ghost writer says he wants to write in dialogue, confine him immediately to perdition. Dialogue is the refuge of the charlatan.

ANGEL
What if you are under a time crunch? You know, the birth of a messiah or the end of a millennium?

HAROLD
Then you can split the job into parts. However, this can be a real management headache. You know, what if Matthew isn't speaking to Mark, and so forth. Writers are like that.

ANGEL
What if the book isn't enough?

HAROLD
Then pick a prophet. I recommend staying away from burning bushes except in major media markets where you can get a lot of TV coverage. Otherwise they're just bad for the environment.

My advice is to pick a talk show host. They're well dressed, and they'll do pretty much anything for ratings.

Harold stands and walks the stage again.

HAROLD
You can even have your talk show host promote your sacred text. This is known in the trade as a televangelist. Be warned: they will take a high percentage of the profits. But as the saying goes, it takes a profit to make a prophet.

ANGEL
And if that doesn't work?

HAROLD
There's one more thing you can try: it is called a—

He writes MIRACLE on the board.

HAROLD
This is also known in the trade as Spooky Action at a Distance.

He writes: S A A A D.

ANGEL
How do you create a miracle?

HAROLD
All it takes is a pair of dice.

He picks a pair of dice out of the quantum void.

ANGEL
Any final suggestions?

HAROLD
Just this: don't lose your sense of humor. Trust me, six days out of seven you'll wish you could just hang out a sign that says God is dead, back on Monday. But that seventh day can be paradise.

So.

Let there be Dark.

Blackout

Act II Scene 7

Setting: The Twilight Zone

At Rise: The hotel room floats in empty space against a backdrop of stars. Harold is standing in front of the door.

The door swings open. Angel is framed in a blinking red light.

HAROLD
Who are you?

ANGEL
The possibility - to pass Without a Moment's Bell - Into Conjecture's presence - Is like a Face of Steel - That suddenly looks into ours With a metallic grin - The Cordiality of Death - Who drills her Welcome in -

Harold holds the door open and she enters. He closes the door and moves toward the window.

Angel opens the blinds. The bright red light is blinking, blinding, on and off.

Harold tries to "go into the light" when the light is on, and steps back when its off.

He does this numerous times.

Angel closes the blinds, goes to him, leads him back to bed.

Blackout

End Act II

ACT III SCENE 1

Setting: The hotel room.

At Rise: The flashing red light is still flashing, alternately illuminating the room dimly and leaving it dark. Harold and Angel are in bed.

Harold sits up in bed, startled.

HAROLD
Wait. Where? Wow.

He gets out of bed. He's not wearing his pants.

HAROLD
Heaven looks a lot like Vegas.

He sees Angel.

HAROLD
Oh my God. I killed her again!

He climbs over her, again starts CPR. As he is giving her mouth-to-mouth resuscitation, her eyes open.

ANGEL
Huh huh huh huhhuh. (This still costs extra).

Harold sits up in shock.

ANGEL
This still costs extra.

HAROLD
You're alive.

He kisses her.

ANGEL
Do you have like a sleeping beauty fetish?

He tries to pull her out of bed.

HAROLD
Here, get up. We have to walk you around.

ANGEL
Yeah, that's just what I want to do.

HAROLD
But what if...

She pushes him away.

ANGEL
I'm okay. Are you okay?

HAROLD
I'm okay. I'm okay. I can't be okay. But I'm okay.

ANGEL
You're okay.

She sits up. She is wearing Harold's shirt. He notices that he is not wearing pants and pulls them on.

HAROLD
What time is it?

He goes to the curtains.

ANGEL
Don't!

He opens the curtains and is again engulfed in blinking red.

ANGEL
This is Vegas. If the sun is blinking, it's night.

He closes the curtains.

HAROLD
Why aren't we dead?

ANGEL
(*sarcastic*)
It's a miracle.

HAROLD
Maybe it was the...you know.

ANGEL
What?

HAROLD
You know...

ANGEL
Give me a hint.

He gestures with his middle finger.

ANGEL
Yeah well fuck you too. Oh, the sex? You think it was the sex? I've raised a lot of things but never the dead.

HAROLD
Maybe the hormones interacted with the chemical structure of the pills, changing them into stimulants.

He sits on the bed next to her.

HAROLD
I did seem stimulated.

ANGEL
And you think it was the pills? I beg your pardon.

HAROLD
There has to be a logical explanation.

She gets out of bed, looking around for something.

ANGEL
I told you, it was a miracle.

HAROLD
Don't be ridiculous.

ANGEL
Obviously I am an angel and God sent me here to spare your life.

Harold sums the histories.

HAROLD
Right. Right? Right!

ANGEL
What?

She finds a boot and sits to put it on.

HAROLD
It fits.

ANGEL
It should.

HAROLD
The hypothesis explains the observed behavior.

ANGEL
What's to explain. It's a boot. I'm putting it on.

HAROLD
But is it verifiable?

ANGEL
It looks like a boot to me.

HAROLD
We need a test.

ANGEL
I could kick you with it.

HAROLD
No. You're an angel. It's a miracle.

ANGEL
I should kick you with it.

She puts the boot on.

HAROLD
What?

ANGEL
Other than the costume, what could possibly lead you to think of me as angelic?

She continues the search.

HAROLD
You performed a miracle. That's pretty convincing evidence.

ANGEL
I performed several things. They were spectacular, but not miraculous.

Harold evaluates the operant possibilities.

HAROLD
We can't automatically assume that you would know you were an angel.

She finds part of her costume and puts it on. She keeps looking.

ANGEL
What, I'm an unconscious angel?

He traces her initial movements back to the door.

HAROLD
You fell.

ANGEL
Oh, now I'm a fallen angel.

HAROLD
You fell and you hit your head so you have angel amnesia. Angelnesia.

ANGEL
I'd like to forget you.

HAROLD
If you're not an angel, how did you know about punctuated equilibrium?

He starts following her around as she searches.

ANGEL
Ballet class?

HAROLD
And summing histories. And Bell's theorem. They don't teach those at ballet class.

ANGEL
When was the last time you took a ballet class?

HAROLD
There's more to you than meets the eye.

ANGEL
And there's more to the eye than meeting me.

> *She finds the other part of her costume and puts it on.*
> *She doffs the shirt and keeps looking.*

HAROLD
That doesn't make sense.

ANGEL
I was changing the subject. You made me nervous.

> *He's on to something. He knows it.*

HAROLD
I made you nervous? Why?

ANGEL
Well, you almost shot me.

HAROLD
But that's not what you meant, was it?

ANGEL
I'd like to change the subject.

HAROLD
I'd like to know.

ANGEL
Why?

> *Now Harold gets nervous.*

HAROLD
I'd like to know if it's the same reason you make me nervous.

> *She considers.*

ANGEL
I'm smart. I don't like people to know. Men. I don't like men to know I'm smart.

HAROLD
Why?

ANGEL
Because. When they find out how smart I am, they leave.

She gets her purse.

HAROLD
That's ridiculous.

She starts to dig through it.

ANGEL
Maybe in your world. In my world they leave.

She pulls out a brush.

HAROLD
I would never leave a woman because she's smart. How smart are you?

She points the brush at him.

ANGEL
Ah ha!

HAROLD
What?

ANGEL
Ah ha!

HAROLD
I wanted to know.

She stands in front of the mirror, brushes her hair.

ANGEL
I knew it.

HAROLD
I was asking a question.

ANGEL
You can't ask that question.

HAROLD
Why not?

She stops brushing and turns.

ANGEL
Because that's like asking what my measurements are.

HAROLD
I don't need to ask that. I can see that for myself.

She turns back and starts brushing again.

ANGEL
Exactly. I want my men like slot machines. Just pull the handle and make 'em spin.

HAROLD
You have to tell me.

ANGEL
Okay. Okay. Okay. I have an IQ of two hundred and sixty.

Harold drops into a chair.

HAROLD
Go on!

ANGEL
Documented.

HAROLD
No way!

ANGEL
It's true.

HAROLD
You're a genius.

ANGEL
Yeah. Yeah.

HAROLD
As I recall from my LATIN class, the word genius comes from the word genie. And genies were the precursors to angels in ancient mythology.

ANGEL
According to whom, Barbara Eden?

She digs around in her purse again.

HAROLD
Why this? You could be anything.

ANGEL
That is a typical academic response.

She pulls out a makeup kit, starts fixing her makeup.

ANGEL
And anyway, the word genius comes from the Latin word gignere, which means to beget.

He's back in detective mode.

HAROLD
Which sounds mighty biblical to me. How do you—

He turns back to confront her suddenly.

HAROLD
Feel?

ANGEL
How do you mean?

HAROLD
It's a simple question. How do you feel? Physically?

She finishes her makeup, puts the kit away.

ANGEL
Not bad, considering my recent suicide. Where is my damn boot?

Again she starts looking for her missing boot.

HAROLD
Exactly.

ANGEL
Exactly what?

HAROLD
You feel fine. Me too. No hangover. No drowsiness. No unpleasant physical effects at all. Right?

ANGEL
Unless you count waking up to you.

HAROLD
But we know that's not possible. With the amount of drugs we took, even if we survived, we should feel something. But we feel fine. Like we got a great night's sleep. Even my breath feels fresh.

ANGEL
Praise the Lord.

He peers at her closely.

HAROLD
You look good too.

ANGEL
Thanks.

HAROLD
How do I look?

ANGEL
Well...

HAROLD
Relatively I mean. Compared to yesterday.

She takes her time, walks around him, looking him over carefully.

ANGEL
Oh. Well. Good actually. Kind of glowing.

HAROLD
Exactly.

ANGEL
Maybe you're the angel.

HAROLD
Let's save that hypothesis for later.

ANGEL
I'll make a note of it.

She starts tossing things around trying to find her boot.

HAROLD
How about mental?

ANGEL
Yes, you seem mental to me.

HAROLD
I mean emotionally? How do you feel? Depressed? Angry? What is your psychological state?

She stops, thinks about it.

ANGEL
Hungry.

HAROLD
That's not a psychological state.

ANGEL
My stomach doesn't know that.

She goes to her purse again.

HAROLD
Exactly.

She digs around the purse.

ANGEL
Stop saying that.

HAROLD
Sorry.

ANGEL
You sound like Sherlock Holmes on lithium.

HAROLD
Exactly. Sorry. But we have a mystery here. We have to solve it.

Finally she pulls out a Twinkie.

ANGEL
Can we eat first?

>   HAROLD
> Would Dr. Watson eat first?
>
>   ANGEL
> No, but he didn't work as hard as I did.

She opens it and takes a bite.

>   HAROLD
> Do you—

He turns back to her again suddenly.

>   HAROLD
> Still want to kill yourself?
>
>   ANGEL
> Not right now, maybe later.

She finishes the Twinkie.

>   HAROLD
> Ex...me too. I feel...great. I feel...happy. I feel...
>
>   ANGEL

She takes out another Twinkie.

Pretty?

>   HAROLD
> Healed. I feel Healed.
>
>   ANGEL
> Can I get an amen?

He gets angry, takes the Twinkie, and points it at her.

>   HAROLD
> This is serious. Something happened. Something important.

ANGEL
Something may have happened. What makes you think it was important?

She takes a bite of the Twinkie in his hand.

ANGEL
There's the real fallacy in your miracle theory. A miracle would never happen to us.

She digs around in her purse for more food.

HAROLD
But it did. It did. Yesterday I was suicidal. Today I am...

ANGEL
Maniacal?

She dumps the contents of the purse on the bed and hunts desperately for another Twinkie.

HAROLD
Healed. I can barely remember how I felt yesterday. It's like it was a different life.

ANGEL
Congratulations.

HAROLD
Let's do it again.

ANGEL
What? Suicide? You just got through...

She sinks dejectedly onto the bed: There are no more Twinkies.

HAROLD
No. Sex. Let's make love.

               ANGEL
Make up your mind. Sex or love?

               HAROLD
Both?

> *She shakes her head.*

               ANGEL
You can't afford both.

> *He looks at himself in the mirror.*

               HAROLD
Do you like me?

> *She looks up at him, puzzled.*

               ANGEL
What does that have to do with—

               HAROLD
I've never asked anyone that before.

> *She looks at his reflection in the mirror.*

               ANGEL
I don't know you.

               HAROLD
You're the first woman I ever committed suicide with.

               ANGEL
The world ends not with a bang but with a preposition.

> *Harold turns to her.*

               HAROLD
Stay with me.

ANGEL
Or should I say proposition?

He kneels.

HAROLD
I mean it. Stay with me.

ANGEL
Ha!

He takes her hand.

HAROLD
I'm serious.

She pulls away.

ANGEL
No.

HAROLD
Why not?

She laughs.

ANGEL
There isn't enough time in the universe to explain all the reasons.

HAROLD
There is no time. There are no reasons. All that's left is a quantum leap of faith.

ANGEL
We did that last night.

She stuffs everything back into the purse.

ANGEL
Oh I see. You think I saved you. So now you want to save me. That's sweet. And really insulting.

She heads for the door.

HAROLD
Stay with me.

She stops.

ANGEL
Stop saying that. Go back to exactly.

He goes to her, stands behind her.

HAROLD
Something happened last night. Whatever it was, I'm convinced that we can't ignore it.

He puts his hands on her shoulders.

HAROLD
We have to respect it, honor it.

She turns.

ANGEL
Forget it.

He doesn't move.

HAROLD
Okay, fine. Let's give it a moment of silence.

She puts down her purse and waits.

ANGEL
Now let's go home.

                    HAROLD
Yes, let's.

She picks up the purse again and starts to leave.

                    ANGEL
Fine.

She stops at the door.

                    ANGEL
What?

                    HAROLD
I'll leave with you.

                    ANGEL
No.

Gently, he takes her purse from her. She lets him.

                    HAROLD
Why are you here?

                    ANGEL
Is this a question of philosophy or location?

He puts her purse back on the dresser.

                    HAROLD
Yes. Why are you here?

                    ANGEL
It was a birthday. Or a joke. Or an accident.

She opens the door. Casino bells blast in.

                    ANGEL
Do you hear those bells? That's the sound of pure probability.

She slams the door closed.

ANGEL
The owners of this place can calculate to the 35th degree how much money each of those machines will make in a year.

She goes to the bucket of coins and takes out a handful.

ANGEL
Yes, you can play a dollar and take home a million. But it isn't luck, it isn't destiny, and it isn't a miracle. It's mathematics. It's probability. That's what runs the world. This world anyway. You're a physicist. You know that better than anyone.

She tosses the coins to him. They fall on the floor. One rolls to the corner.

HAROLD
That's the whole point. That's what I'm trying to tell you.

He picks up the coins.

HAROLD
Probability doesn't mean things are random. This is what they couldn't understand, at the conference.

He goes for the coin in the corner.

HAROLD
In quantum physics, we talk in probabilities, because we can't know the underlying mechanism.

He finds the coin and holds it up. It glimmers in the light.

HAROLD
Take the slot machine. You and I don't know how it works. But we know it does.

He shifts the coins from hand to hand, like a machine paying out.

HAROLD
And because probability works, we know it's not random. It's controlled. By something.

He goes back to her, at the dresser.

HAROLD
I know one thing. You're here because something brought you here. I don't know what. I don't know why.

He places the coins in her hand.

HAROLD
I'm willing to spend the rest of my life finding out. But I can't do it without you.

She drops the coins back in the bucket.

ANGEL
Stop it.

HAROLD
Why?

ANGEL
There was no miracle.

HAROLD
But we're alive.

She laughs.

ANGEL
We were never going to die.

HAROLD
The pills—

ANGEL
Weren't sleeping pills.

HAROLD
I don't understand.

> *She gets the purse, takes out the bottle of pills.*

ANGEL
They were breath mints.

> *She takes one.*

HAROLD
Breath mints?

> *She blows her breath at him.*

ANGEL
Important part of my business.

> *He takes the bottle from her.*

HAROLD
But they were in a prescription bottle.

ANGEL
Childproof cap. Stays closed when I have to make a quick getaway.

> *He tastes one.*

HAROLD
Well at least that explains why my breath feels minty fresh.

> *She takes the bottle of pills, screws the cap back on. She drops the bottle, and sees her boot under the dresser. She retrieves it and sits on the bed to put it on.*

HAROLD
You're leaving.

ANGEL
Yes.

HAROLD
Why?

ANGEL
It's what I do.

She starts to pull on the boot.

HAROLD
Don't.

ANGEL
First you don't want me to get undressed, now you don't want me to get dressed.

HAROLD
Why did you have sex with me?

ANGEL
I wanted to go out with a bang?

HAROLD
Tell me.

She stops.

ANGEL
I had to distract you until you fell asleep.

HAROLD
I don't buy it.

ANGEL
Someone did.

She pulls off the boot and throws it at him. He dodges.

ANGEL
Don't you know what I am?

HAROLD
You're an angel.

She laughs.

HAROLD
You're an angel to me.

ANGEL
De gustibus non disputandem est.

She retrieves the boot.

ANGEL
I was paid for, Harold.

HAROLD
No, you knew it was a mistake. I didn't pay you. You knew. But you stayed. And we made love.

She throws the boot at him, hits him this time. He goes down.

ANGEL
We fucked, Harold. It's what I do.

She goes to him, helps him up and to the bed.

HAROLD
What does that mean? It's what I do.

ANGEL
I'm a performer. I come. I perform. I leave. I can't explain it any better than that. It's what I do.

Harold sits up in bed.

HAROLD
I remember. In the dream.

She gets some very watery ice.

ANGEL
What dream?

She wraps it in the pillowcase.

HAROLD
Maybe it wasn't a dream. Maybe it was a near death experience.

She holds it to his head.

ANGEL
You weren't near death. It was a near sex experience.

HAROLD
Whatever. I remember. It's what you do.

She takes his hand, puts it up to hold the ice.

ANGEL
What are you talking about? What dream?

HAROLD
A dream I had after...we fell asleep. You were there and I was there.

ANGEL
Was there a tin man and a cowardly lion?

HAROLD
It was an audition.

She drops the ice in his lap.

HAROLD
Ahhh! You danced. You were wonderful. So beautiful. Beautiful flowing light. You danced as if God were watching.

ANGEL
God is always watching.

HAROLD
You think so?

She looks up.

ANGEL
God I hope not.

Harold winces.

HAROLD
If he's watching, why doesn't he do something?

ANGEL
I'd have to kill you to tell you.

HAROLD
You danced like an angel.

She gets up, moves away from him.

ANGEL
I have that dream all the time.

HAROLD
Did you have it last night?

ANGEL
Yes.

HAROLD
But something was different, wasn't it?

ANGEL
Yes.

HAROLD
It was the music.

ANGEL
I'd never heard it before.

Harold reaches over to the CD player.

HAROLD
It sounded like this.

He turns on the CD player. Thus Spake Zarathustra fills the room.

HAROLD
Do you remember anything else? Any other dreams?

ANGEL
I remember you. You were teaching or something.

HAROLD
Yes. I was. Divinity school. What did I talk about?

ANGEL
You went on for an eternity.

HAROLD
Exactly.

ANGEL
You were talking about universes and dancing and...

HAROLD
Yes?

ANGEL
Miracles.

She looks at him.

ANGEL
We had the same dreams.

He nods.

ANGEL
How is that possible?

HAROLD
Miracles.

Now she is the detective.

ANGEL
It must have been the pills.

Harold blissfully counters her.

HAROLD
Breath mints.

ANGEL
The sex.

HAROLD
Spectacular. Not miraculous.

ANGEL
This is spooky.

HAROLD
Action at a distance. Exactly.

She retrieves her boot again.

ANGEL
I'm getting out of here.

HAROLD
So, you've thought this through completely, I imagine, like the intelligent woman you are, if you don't mind my using that term.

She sits to pull it on.

ANGEL
Yes. Of course. Completely. Why?

HAROLD
I know that this all seems like some accident. But it's not.

He gets up carefully and walks to the board.

HAROLD
It's a miracle. And I can prove it.

ANGEL
How?

He pauses for a moment, then erases everything.

HAROLD
How many hotel rooms are there in Las Vegas?

ANGEL
51,462.

Harold stares at her.

ANGEL
What? I haven't been in all of them. It's on the website.

He shrugs and writes 51462 on the board.

HAROLD
That means that the chance you would enter this room is 51462 to one.

ANGEL
If you say so.

HAROLD
So how long have we been in here?

ANGEL
About 5 hours?

HAROLD
Okay. 5 hours, that's 300 minutes, that's 18,000 seconds. So the chance that you would knock on my hotel door at exactly that second is—

He writes the next figures on the board too.

HAROLD
51,462 times 18,000 which is--.

ANGEL
926,326,000.

HAROLD
Right. Now, the chance that I would be on a chair with a gun at exactly the same second out of those five hours is—

He writes again.

HAROLD
926,136,000 times 18,000 which is about—

He looks at her.

ANGEL
16,670,448,000,000.

HAROLD
To one. So assuming you do this 4 times a day--

ANGEL
That's a good day.

HAROLD
300 days a year—

ANGEL
That's a good year.

HAROLD
Which is 1200 times a year, you would have to dance for—

ANGEL
13,892,040,000.

HAROLD
Years to find someone else like me. Which is almost exactly the amount of time since the beginning of the universe. This is proof. This day was planned from the beginning of the universe. It's a miracle.

He writes MIRACLE on the board and circles it.

ANGEL
You don't plan miracles.

HAROLD
You mean we don't.

She edges for the door.

ANGEL
Okay I'll agree that it's a miracle if you promise it won't happen again for another 13 billion years.

HAROLD
Deal.

ANGEL
Look. My knocking on this door was an accident. The fact that I did it just in time was an accident. The fact that we're still alive is probably just…bad luck for both of us.

He points to the board.

HAROLD
But what if it's not?

ANGEL
It is.

HAROLD
Look, I've spent my life studying accidents. That's what quantum physics is all about.

He draws bells in the corners again.

HAROLD
But what if there really is a purpose. And miracles. And angels.

ANGEL
And Santa Claus and the Easter Bunny.

She takes the marker from him.

ANGEL
Lives don't change because of one incident. Tomorrow night I'll be in another hotel room with someone else. Tomorrow night you'll be in another hotel room shooting someone else.

HAROLD
If miracles lasted forever, they wouldn't be miracles.

She points the marker at his head.

ANGEL
Remember why you came here.

He takes the marker back.

HAROLD
I came here to meet you. Where else could I meet you?

She laughs.

ANGEL
Me?

HAROLD
I have to understand.

ANGEL
Anywhere.

HAROLD
It's what I do.

He picks up the gun.

HAROLD
You can't leave. If we go, we go together. One way or another.

ANGEL
You don't mean that.

HAROLD
Don't I?

She takes the gun.

ANGEL
No. Because there was only one bullet in the gun.

He sighs.

HAROLD
I was hoping you'd forgotten.

ANGEL
You're the kind of man who wouldn't want anyone else to get hurt by accident.

Angel puts the gun down.

ANGEL
I won't ever forget that.

He takes her hand.

HAROLD
Stay with me, Ellie.

ANGEL
Tell you what. Let's flip for it. Heads I stay, tails I go.

HAROLD
You can't be serious.

ANGEL
You wanted a test.

HAROLD
You want to decide our lives on a coin toss?

She gets a silver dollar from the bucket.

ANGEL
Look at the decisions you've made in your life. Wouldn't you have been better off flipping a coin?

She flips the coin in the air a few times.

HAROLD
Okay.

ANGEL
Are you game?

HAROLD
Do I have a choice?

ANGEL
Do you think you do?

HAROLD
Go ahead.

ANGEL
Call it.

She flips the coin.

HAROLD
Heads.

She catches the coin and looks at it, then looks at him.

HAROLD
Just one question.

ANGEL
What?

HAROLD
How many angels can dance on the head of a pin?

She laughs.

ANGEL
An infinite number, Harold.

She kisses him gently.

ANGEL
One after another.

Harold gets her wings from the easel.

HAROLD
You're wrong. I'm certain.

ANGEL
Certain? Why?

He hands the wings to her.

                        HAROLD
There is only one Angel.

> *She puts her purse and wings down by the door, then moves to the dresser to check herself in the mirror, sees the coins in the bucket.*

                        ANGEL
When did you win all these coins?

> *Harold sits on the bed.*

                        HAROLD
I was sitting at a slot machine, trying to decide whether to go through with it. I put a coin in. Pulled the handle. Watched the wheels. Put a coin in. Pulled the handle. Watched the wheels. And finally I thought: why should I keep playing a game I know in time I'm going to lose?

> *Angel takes the bucket of coins over to Harold.*

                        ANGEL
What else is there to do in Vegas?

> *She walks to the door, puts on her wings, then opens the door. Casino bells blast in.*

> *She gestures like a dealer leaving a blackjack table.*

                        ANGEL
Good luck, Harold.

> *As she leaves, the door closes almost tight.*

> *Harold sits there for a while, not knowing what to do. He picks up a coin from the bucket.*

HAROLD
Heads I go after her. Tails I kill myself.

He pauses, then he puts the coin back in the bucket. He stands. Then he throws the entire bucket of coins up in the air. Coins go everywhere. When they hit the ground, Harold looks them over intently. Then he chooses one.

HAROLD
Heads it is.

He opens the door. Casino bells blast in.

HAROLD
Listen to the bells.

He rushes out. After he's gone, the CD player starts to play Thus Spake Zarathustra.

Blackout

The End

STEPHEN EVANS

Playwright's Note

As our understanding (such as it is) of cosmology changes, the number assigned to the age of the universe may also change. Currently it is 13.8 billion years. In the twenty years I have been working on this play, the number has changed three or four times, to my knowledge.

If it changes again, as seems likely, feel free to change the number of hotel rooms in Vegas to make Harry's calculation come out right. Assuming it does. If I had been any good at math, I would have been a physicist myself.

STEPHEN EVANS

About the Playwright

Stephen Evans is a playwright and the author. Find him online at:

https://www.istephenevans.com/

https://www.facebook.com/iStephenEvans

https://twitter.com/iStephenEvans

STEPHEN EVANS

Books by Stephen Evans

Fiction:
The Island of Always Series:
    The Marriage of True Minds
    Let Me Count the Ways
    My Winter World
Whose Beauty is Past Change
The Marriage Gift
Paradox
The Mind of a Writer and other Fables
The Next Joy and the Next: A Mythology
Some Version of This is Funny: Jokes and Observations

Non-Fiction:
Prolegomena to Any Future Vacation
Funny Thing Is: A Guide to Understanding Comedy
The Laughing String: Thoughts on Writing
Layers of Life: Essays and Aphorisms
Liebestraum

STEPHEN EVANS

Plays:

The Visitation Quartet:
   The Ghost Writer
   Spooky Action at a Distance
   Tourists
   Monuments

Generations   (with Morey Norkin and Michael Gilles)

As You Like It   (by William Shakespeare, adapted by Stephen Evans)

The Glass Door (An Adaptation of Hedda Gabler by Henrik Ibsen))

Verse:

Limerosity
Limerositus

Sonets from the Chesapeke

A Look from Winter

STEPHEN EVANS

Stephen Evans

www.ingramcontent.com/pod-product-compliance
Lightning Source LLC
Chambersburg PA
CBHW020312010526
44107CB00001B/71